PET LIBRARY'S

Poodle

Guide

PET LIBRARY'S

Poodle

Guide

by Barbara Lockwood

and

Margaret Sheldon

England

THE PET LIBRARY LTD

The Pet Library Ltd.,
Subsidiary of Sternco In-
dustries Inc., 600 South
Fourth Street, Harrison,
N.J. Exclusive Canadian
Distributor: Hartz Moun-
tain Pet Supplies Limited,
1125 Talbot Street, St.
Thomas, Ontario, Canada.
Exclusive United King-
dom Distributor: The Pet
Library (London) Ltd.,
30 Borough High Street,
London S.E. 1.

© 1968 Barbara Lock-
wood and Margaret
Sheldon (England).

Printed in the Netherlands

ISBN 0-87826-420-5

Table of Contents

The Clown Clip – The Hillbilly Clip – The Sailor Boy
Clip – The Cowboy Clip – The Baby Doll Clip

Cover picture: Sally Anne Thompson

PHOTOGRAPH LOANED BY MRS. HAROLD COX

The late Sir Winston Churchill with his brown Poodle, "Rufus," who for many years was his constant and much-loved companion.

I A Man's Best Friend

So you are going to get yourself a dog? There may be many reasons why this was not possible until now, and consequently you have waited à long time, even years, before fulfilling your ambition. On the other hand, you may have owned many dogs, and the time has come round again when you are planning to get a new one.

The real dog lover should have his own dog, because for such a person life is not complete without one. A dog has a lot to give at almost every period throughout his life and ours. As a child, the thrill of owning a puppy is wonderful; to wake up on Christmas morning or on a birthday to find a tiny puppy sticking out of your father's pocket and to learn that this is a special gift for you, can be an exciting experience. It is better than any other gift could possibly be; moreover, such a present means a child's first introduction to responsibility and he or she must learn a great many precepts before being ready to take over the ownership of a dog.

Later in this book there is a special chapter to tell children how to look after a puppy properly. Then, as he grows older, what school-child does not experience the happiness of the warm and vociferous welcome he receives from his dog when he returns home. During the painful period of adolescence, when most young people suffer from depression and moodiness, what better companion can be found than one's own dog always at hand, a sympathetic and loving companion.

Then, in turn, there is the thrill of giving one's own children their first dog and experiencing vicariously the joy and happiness of having a real life companion. As retirement draws near, again the dog is an indispensable part of one's life, for then there is leisure for perhaps breeding and showing dogs, and certainly more time for walking, the pleasure of which is enhanced a hundredfold if one owns a dog. And so on to the saddest time of life, when old age has caught up with us, and we realize that we can no longer look after a dog properly, and know we must not, for selfish reasons, keep a dog unless we are physically and mentally able to tend him as he should be tended, and indeed, as he has a right to expect.

But we are racing through the years too fast. Undoubtedly, to the real dog lover no period of his life from childhood to old age is complete without a canine friend and companion, and, in fact, to many such dog lovers, life simply cannot be contemplated without a dog around.

The Burglar's Foe

Dogs have so much to give. There is no better protection than a dog whether it be a German Shepherd trained to use his teeth on command, or the tiny Yorkshire Terrier who will, with his bark, let everyone know that danger is imminent. The dog is far more efficient than any burglar alarm. It has been noticed, in this day and age of violence, that a person attacked or assaulted on a lonely road, or when alone in a house, was seldom accompanied by a dog. It does not necessarily need to be a guard dog, for any breed of dog, large or small, will make a great deal of noise if his owner is molested or in trouble. The sudden noise will draw immediate attention to the crime, and the culprit will be away before he has completed his violence or atrocity.

How often does the juvenile delinquent own a dog? One never sees a dog attached to a gang of youngsters who are bent on mischief. Ownership of a dog in these circumstances is a disadvantage, for a dog provides one of the best means of identification in a police line-up, as recognition of his owner by scent will be immediate. Therefore, those who live on the wrong side of the law, or even on the fringe, prefer not to have a dog. There is the exception of those who dabble in poaching, for there a good killer, hunter or retriever is a valuable asset. The well-known Dickens character, Bill Sykes, could not have managed without his dog! But if all the young boys in "Oliver Twist," who were employed by Fagin, had owned a dog, the thieves' den would not have operated for long! This is, however, a negative aspect. On the positive side, care of a dog teaches a youngster concern for others. It is difficult to be anti-society once one has learned kindness and thoughtfulness. Owning a dog is a lifelong lesson in responsibility.

The Working Dog

How many blind people owe their very existence to a guide dog? What inestimable service such a dog has given to people so sadly handicapped in this way. How many totally incapacitated people have a reason for living because of the companionship given to them by their dogs. How many lonely or exiled folk rely on their dogs to make life tolerable.

Then there are the working farm dogs who manage their flocks of sheep with such gentleness and yet with the utmost control, and take an obvious delight in their own special work. What would the farmer do without his working sheep dog? There is no doubt that the dog has served man faithfully in so many ways, and in return could expect protection from all that might harm him, comfort in

A Poodle will suit almost anybody, will adopt itself to almost every circumstance and condition. They come in all sizes and all colors, and can be clipped to almost any shape.

his living conditions, and a return of that love which he so unstintingly and so unquestioningly gives to his master. But does the dog always receive that which is his by right? Sadly enough, the answer must be "not always". Therefore, anyone who wants a dog must not approach the prospect lightly, for a dog is not a toy to be played with for a few weeks and then discarded, nor a pet to be groomed and walked and well-fed only when he is new. There is far more to it than that. He must receive lifelong care and consideration, and loving attention, and it is hoped that this book will help prospective dog owners to learn how best to look after their dogs – to make their inter-twined lives a time of happiness and security.

The Right Breed

So, having made up your mind that a dog must be obtained, you must consider what type of dog would be most suited to your own way of life. For instance, do you fancy a large, strong watchdog who will be the perfect guard? A German Shepherd, a Doberman, a Bull Terrier, a Boxer, or an Airedale could all be considered. But they will need a lot of room, and a lot of food! If you live in a small apartment or have only limited means, these are points that should be considered.

Perhaps you want a dog who will enter into your particular sporting activities, in which case maybe a Cocker Spaniel, a Golden Retriever, a Beagle or a working terrier would be suitable. Perhaps you are a great walker, then a Wire-haired terrier, a Dalmatian, or a Corgi might appeal. Equally, you may not be in the least active, and may want your dog to be content to sit by the fireside, able to function with very little exercise, and particularly happy when he can sit on your lap. Then a Toy dog may be indicated – a Pekingese or a Maltese Terrier, a Chihuahua or a Papillon – but here it must be stressed that many so-called "lap dogs" have been burdened with that label arbitrarily, and many small Toy dogs enjoy a long walk and a chase through the woods and fields as much as do their brethren who wear a label of "toughness" around their collars!

Why a Poodle?

Having considered all these breeds with their various advantages and disadvantages, there is one breed which so far has not been mentioned, and that is the Poodle. Surely here is the answer, for a Poodle will suit almost everybody, will adapt itself to almost every circumstance and condition. Poodles come in three sizes. The Standard Poodle stands between 23 and 28 inches at the shoulder, and weighs about 40 lbs. There is his smaller brother, the Miniature Poodle, who should measure under 15 inches from shoulder to ground, and weigh around 15 to 20 pounds. The smallest size, the Toy Poodle, measures under 10 inches at the shoulder and weighs around 6 to 10 pounds. In England and some European countries, the Toy Poodle may be taller, measuring under 11 inches at the shoulder. In Germany, Poodles come in four sizes: the Toy, anything up to 11 inches; the Zwerg (dwarf) to 15 inches; the Miniature, up to 20 inches, and the Standard, anything above 20.

But why is the Poodle such a popular breed? What inspires so many owners to choose this particular dog? Is it just a fashion, or is there more to it than that? We think the answer can only be given by someone who has owned this breed, and can sum up the characteristics which have such a bearing on the continued popularity of Poodles. It is a fact that no other breed has remained so popular for so many years at a stretch, so surely this must be due to some attribute that the Poodle alone possesses. This attribute can be summed up in a couple of words – *delightful temperament.* One has only to own a Poodle to know what grand dogs they are. In no way are they the spoiled lap dogs that some people imagine.

The Poodle is definitely Dog-Plus, and the "Plus" stands for better than average canine intelligence. A Poodle really thinks, and works out situations and ways around those situations with almost uncanny (and un-canine!) thinking power. He is not always an angel, and can chew up his master's slippers or chase the neighbor's cat with the best of them – but who wants a plaster saint for a dog? He is sometimes very obstinate and intends to get his own way by any means. He is undoubtedly vain and loves to look smart and well-groomed. But the Poodle has a wonderful sense of humor

LOUISE VAN DER MEID

The Poodle loves to travel. Apricot Toy Poodle owned by Glamor Manor of California.

In England, and also in America, the Miniature and the Toy Poodles have been the most popular breeds for many years, topping the Kennel Club registrations. Here, Mrs. Campbell-Inglis is judging the best Toy, the best Miniature, and the best Standard for the final award of Best in show at the International Poodle Club Champion Show in London, England.

and can always share a joke. He can be quiet and relaxed when desired, but equally game to take a ten mile walk with you if you feel in the mood.

A Poodle is usually an excellent car traveler, welcome in any hotel, motel, caravan or boat and, provided he is properly trained from puppyhood, will stay quiet in a car or room by himself, having the sense to know that it is required of him and that you will surely come back for him in good time. He is a good mixer with others of his kind and certainly not a fighter, preferring to turn away from the offender with dignity. He is polite to strangers but does not hurl himself effusively at any caller – he likes to get to know his friends, both human and canine, and then will give incredible love and devotion, and seldom forgets them even though they have not met for some time. Certainly, as a general rule, the Poodle has a gay and

15

friendly nature which stems from generations of good temperament handed down from the original which was a large Standard Poodle.

It is unusual to find a snappy or bad-tempered Poodle, and when one does come across such a dog it usually means either that the strain from which he stems has been indiscriminately bred (that is, careful choice of well dispositioned sires and dames has been disregarded down through the generations, and a bad streak has been propagated over the years – a most foolish and short-sighted breeding policy), or one finds that the human element was at fault in the handling of such a Poodle from the nest onwards, and in this case one can hardly blame the dog for that which environment wrought.

When buying a puppy, either for a companion or for the show ring, it is wise to insure that its breeder has given great thought and care to breeding judiciously only from those dogs whose temperaments are a hundred per cent – not only just in the case of the sire and dam, but also in many previous generations. Physical fitness has a bearing on good temperament, and only the dog who is physically fit and bred from generations of carefully reared, healthy, and well cared for Poodles is going to be temperamentally sound and at ease in his mind, not distorted by inherited inhibitions and fears.

In England, the Miniature and Toy Poodles have been the most popular breeds for many years, topping the English Kennel Club registrations. We have yet to meet someone who has owned a Poodle and not felt that this breed transcends all other breeds. Once having owned a Poodle, one realizes that no other breed has quite the same intelligence, character, or devotion, nor such a tremendous capacity for companionship.

Which Size to Choose

To fill the need for a watchdog, choose a Standard Poodle. His alertness and keen sense of smell will lead him to recognize danger immediately, and his weight, build and speed will deter any prospective criminal.

For generations in England, France, and Germany the Poodle has been trained to work with the gun by those who wanted a dog to accompany them on sporting pursuits. His sagacity and intelligence make him a splendid contender in the obedience ring, while his tremendous dignity and elegance take him to the top in the beauty ring.

For those who do not have too much room in their homes, the compact Miniature Poodle is ideal. Here is a dog who is alert enough to make a fine watchdog, and one who is extremely intelligent and easy to train. He is ideal in the Show Ring because again he moves with such elegance and so obviously adores showing off! The "Mini" is a dog small enough to take anywhere on vacation, for there are few things a Miniature Poodle enjoys more than car riding, camping or boating. He is not in the least aggressive and never picks a quarrel, and he is always ready and willing to join in anything at any time in any place, so long as his owner wants him to.

Finally, there is the tiny Toy Poodle who is again a valuable watchdog, for he will always be the first to sniff impending danger. He is a tiny dog, easy to slip under your arm and take anywhere, one who needs very little exercise, and can manage quite well on a short walk around the block twice a day. He is a small dog who eats little, comparatively speaking, and one who becomes completely devoted to his owner to the exclusion of everyone else. Certainly, a midget dog is admirably suited to the less active owner and to those who are getting on in years, but he is equally a dog

The "Mini" is a dog small enough to take anywhere, he is not in the least aggressive and never picks a quarrel, he is always ready and willing to join in anything at any time in any place.

with enough energy and spirit to compete with the Miniature Poodle in every circumstance if given the chance.

Toy Poodles are also popular with the young miss of today. Even a girl on the go can always find room for her diminutive companion, and the opportunity to dress the hair of her complaisant dog holds an appeal hard to resist. It is really amazing, the number of big strong men who enjoy the company of a tiny Toy. Many women when purchasing a puppy say, "My husband can't stand small dogs but we just don't have room for a big one." Invariably those same men, once they've overcome their initial resistance, find the spindly little Toy Poodle all dog and everything they ever wanted.

Poodles have a very great advantage as house pets, as they are one of the few breeds that can safely be kept in a house with persons suffering from asthma because there is less shedding of skin scales from them than from some of the other breeds.

They do have one slight disadvantage in that the various styles into which they must be clipped cost money when done by the expert in the grooming parlor; but in this book, among many other things, we shall show you how to deal competently with the grooming and clipping of your Poodle to the advantage of your pocketbook. On the other hand to the artistically inclined, what better way to express himself than by shaping his Poodle's coat!

Therefore, having investigated the many assets which the Poodle can bring to your home, surely this breed can be the only choice for anyone who is embarking on the delight and pleasure of owning a dog. There are few breeds that have so much to give, that are so adaptable to any set of circumstances, and who will give you, his owner, such lasting and marvelous companionship. Therefore, get yourself a Poodle right away – tomorrow is too late. You will never regret it.

These little scamps are so adorable that it's hard to punish them. However, for their own good (and yours) they must learn not to chew slippers.

II Poodle History

A great deal has been written regarding the history of the Poodle, but not all authors are in agreement. There is no doubt that the Poodle was one of the earliest hunting dogs, and most writers put the early 1500's as the date when the Poodle first became known. However, Mr. Howard Price, an authority, tells us that he has been able "to trace evidence of Roman and Greek coins which clearly show a dog with a large lion-like mane and hind quarters clipped short." He also claims that "little Poodles were represented on some monuments about the time of the Emperor Augustus, approximately A.D. 30," and that is certainly going back a long time.

The Irish Water Spaniel (left) and the European or Portuguese Water Dog have probably figured in the ancestry of our Poodle.

Poodles Were Water Dogs

However, to start a little nearer to our own time, there seems to be no doubt that the Poodle originally came from a mixture of water dogs which were to be found in various European countries, principally Russia, France, Germany and Spain. A connection with early Poodles is apparent, for there is a very marked similarity between the European Water Dog, the Portuguese Water Dog and the Irish Water Spaniel.

In the drawings it will be seen that the early Poodles were usually depicted with a large mane of hair covering the neck, shoulders and chest of the dog, together with long hair fringes on the ears, and a profuse top-knot sometimes tied up with ribbon so that they could be distinguished when working in the reeds. The coat was clipped close to the body from the end of the ribs, down over the loins, buttocks and thighs. Both fore and hind legs were clipped close although a circle of hair was left around both ankles and both hocks. The tail, which was undocked in those days was also clipped but bore a tuft of hair on the end. As will be seen, the Portuguese Water Dog (the Cao d'Aqua) wore very much the same style, and obviously this style was adopted by both breeds to facilitate their progress through water – a fact in favor of the theory that these two water dogs probably had a common origin.

The Irish Water Spaniel had no similar clipping style, but his coat texture very much resembles the true, correct texture of the Poodle coat, and also his head and ears greatly resemble the Poodle. Therefore, it seems reasonable to assume that this trio of water dogs were the ancestors of the Poodle as we know him today.

Reproduction of the front page of a Parliamentary broadsheet dated 1642
referring to the famous white Poodle owned by Prince Rupert. Photograph
kindly lent by Mr. Stanley Dangerfield.

About the middle of the sixteenth century, the name *Pudel* became known in both Russia and Germany and was used to describe a large dog employed extensively for hunting water fowl, known to be an extremely clever retriever. The breed gradually made its way into Holland and Belgium where it became known as the Poedel, and then into France with the name of Barbet. Mr. L. E. Naylor, in his book "Poodles," tells us that the word Pudel stems from the German verb *puddeln,* meaning to "splash in water". This again points to the fact that Poodles were water dogs. The early Russian Poodles varied greatly in size, from a giant hunting dog weighing as much as eighty pounds, down to tiny little dogs weighing only as much as the present day Toys, but they all seemed to be classified under the heading of Pudel. The Germans, however, quickly graded these dogs into the *Gross Pudel,* the *Mittlere Pudel,* and the *Kleine Pudel,* meaning great, medium and tiny.

Until about 1930, the breed was always referred to as the French Poodle, though there seems little or no evidence that France can claim this breed as its own. The word "French" seems to have been dropped in modern times, and is now seldom heard.

Antique China Poodle figurines. In the center is a beautifully-fashioned Rockingham model while on either side are Staffordshire China models produced in the mid-1800's in England.

Prince Rupert's "Boye"

It is commonly believed that Prince Rupert was the first person to bring a Poodle to England, in the mid-seventeenth century. The Prince, after his release from imprisonment in Europe, came to England to join King Charles I in his battles with the Roundheads, bringing with him his large white Poodle, "Boye." This dog was supposed to possess supernatural powers, to be able to speak a variety of languages, and to be quite impervious to death. "Boye" became a considerable annoyance to the Roundheads, chiefly because he was such a favorite with King Charles and his court. Mr. Howard Price states,

> This was not lost on the puritanical Roundheads who issued pamphlets to this effect, adding that Boye was possessed of supernatural powers in league with the Pope and the Devil. It is in this first pamphlet that America is called on to handle the Poodle... "for it is impossible to destroy him, until the Colonies of New England come in to help us; they know how to order these Dog-Witches better far than we. Brotherly assistance may perhaps do something".

The gallant Poodle, "Boye", died in battle on Marston Moor in 1644.

There seems to be only sparse mention of the Poodle again until the beginning of the 1800's when the *Sportsman's Repository* was published, and this referred to the Poodle as a breed of water dog. But from 1820, for the next eighty years, wordy battles in print were continually taking place as to whether the Water Dog and the Poodle were one and the same. Finally, it was decided that they were.

In the early 1800's there began to appear the beautiful little Rockingham porcelain Poodles which are so prized by collectors nowadays, and just slightly later came the Staffordshire model Poodles, but these are not really so elegant or enchanting as the Rockingham figurines.

Circus Poodles

The typical traditional lion clip of the Poodle is said by many enthusiasts to have been inspired by the French clowns who worked their Poodles in circuses. The bracelets, anklets and pompons on

Silver Toy Poodle sired by International Champion Thornlea Silver Souvenir. Silver puppies are born black. The color develops as they mature. When the face and feet are clipped, as we see here, the silver color beneath is exposed.

head and tail were supposed to have matched the pompons on the traditional dress of these clowns. But surely the true origin of this clip stems from the early days of the European Water Dogs which as we noted was adopted solely to facilitate more ease of movement through water and rushes, and was only exaggerated by the French clowns who embellished the style adding pompons on the shaven part on the loins. This rather more outlandish style enhanced the acts, and in the late 1800's and early 1900's nearly every circus had a Poodle act. But this did not greatly help the prestige of the Poodle for they were apt to be looked upon as trick dogs, buffoons, and the companions of itinerant players. It is hard for us today when actors are so lionized, to realize in what low esteem they were held during the Middle Ages. Actors were all considered dishonest, and actresses immoral. This contempt even extended to the animals associated with them, and for a time had an adverse effect on the popularity of the Poodle.

Miss Clara Bowring tells us in "The Book of the Poodle" that Poodles really came to England in quite large numbers after the Napoleonic Wars, for the soldiers returning from Germany and France became very fond of the German *Pudel* and the French *Caniche* and brought them back in considerable numbers as pets for their families. The French name, *Caniche,* comes from the word "canard" which again adds a pointer to the fact that Poodles were used extensively for duck retrieving.

Curly and Corded

However, by about 1880, Poodles were being exhibited in the English show ring, and were divided into two categories – the Curly Poodle and the Corded Poodle. This was only a distinction of coat for the size, structure and conformation of both varieties were identical. It was simply that the coat of the Curly Poodle was brushed out more or less as is the Poodle of today, and was trimmed to a neat style, whereas the coat of the Corded Poodle was allowed to grow naturally, and the hair often attained a great length, the strands being twisted into cords and dressed with oil. The hair was never brushed or combed. Because of this, Corded Poodles never became universally popular, for the procedure involved too much hard work and the odor and mess were unpleasant.

Truffle Dogs

Poodles are often referred to as "Truffle" dogs. The truffle is the king of the succulent mushroom. It grows underground and is much sought after as a culinary delicacy. The best quality truffles are to be found in certain districts of France and are sometimes very large, weighing as much as eight to ten pounds each; they are in their best condition from late Autumn until about March. (Truffles are occasionally found in England but they are inferior in taste and weight.) Because of their extremely sensitive noses, Poodles have an uncanny aptitude for locating these underground fungi, and therefore they were extensively used for this work. Their sense of smell would direct the Poodles to where truffles were growing; they would then paw the ground and start to dig up the earth, by which time the master would have arrived, and gently unearthing the clump of truffles, send his Poodle on to locate the next likely spot. Before it was discovered that Poodles had this gift for truffle hunting the pig was used. This animal had a passion for the succulent truffle and would root energetically until a clump was found. However, the pig is a greedy animal and also extremely quick. He usually managed to swallow most of the truffles before the human truffle gatherer arrived. Poodles, on the other hand, seemed to have no desire to eat the truffles and were therefore much better.

A beautiful bronze model of a Poodle, dated about 1775, the photograph kindly lent by Mr. Stanley Dangerfield, English Championship Show Judge.

The Poodle in Art

A word about the Poodle in art must not be omitted, for he has always been an excellent subject for the artist in many mediums, and through the ages he has been painted, carved, etched and modeled. One of the earliest works connected with Poodles is the painting by Franz Snyder about 1595, which shows a water dog attacking geese. Then there is the Parliamentary Broadsheet dated 1642 referring to Prince Rupert and his white Pudel, "Boye," which can be seen in the Print Room of the British Museum in London.

Another early painting is that by Jan Steen entitled "The Dancing Dog" (about 1660), showing a small white Poodle dancing on his hind legs in typical Poodle style. There is a very lovely bronze model of French origin of a Poodle dated 1775, which is now in America. Then there are two most amusing prints by Le Bon Genre the first of which shows "Munito, the Calculating Poodle," a white Poodle cleverly picking out numbered cards on command from his trainer with astonished onlookers standing by. This print is dated 1817. The second print is dated a year later, and is called "The Toy Poodle at Dinner." This shows a tiny white Poodle, beautifully groomed and bedecked, sitting up to the table and being offered the wishbone from the chicken on the end of his mistress' fork. The lady is extravagantly dressed, and the table is well laden with good food and wine, but a pathetic social touch is added as a somewhat timid maid is depicted seated in the corner, eating what appears to be a slice of bread from a napkin spread on her lap.

Perhaps the best known Poodle lithograph is that of Chalon's "Les Tondeuses de Chiens" (1820) which must surely depict the forerunner of the modern grooming parlor. Here are two Frenchwomen seated on upturned boxes busily clipping the Poodles lying on their laps. The attitudes of the Poodles are excellent, if somewhat inelegant, as they are lying on their backs and suffering the ministrations of the women with apparent distaste. Two other Poodles are chained at one side in the lithograph, obviously having completed their beauty treatment, while in a barred travelling box are two more Poodles waiting their turn. The manipulator of the scissors is shaded by a very large umbrella, and a nice touch is the large rent in its fabric.

There is another amusing etching called "Innocent Amusements" by Theodore Lane, dated 1820, showing the proverbial maiden lady

"Les Tondeuses de Chiens," a colored lithograph engraving by J. J. Chalon, dated 1820, from the collection owned by Mr. Stanley Dangerfield. This shows the equivalent of the modern Poodle Parlor, here operated by the women "barbers" of France in the market place.

engaged in grooming her white Poodle on a table. The Poodle is in Lion trim and his hair is twisted in a number of curlpapers. On the table are various lotions and scents, and on the floor is a china jug and basin. A lovebird is perched on the screen watching the proceedings.

Many will be familiar with the bizarre drawings of Cruikshank, and will know the one called "Monstrosities." Here the main figure is not a Poodle, but one does appear in the right-hand bottom corner. He is a deliciously presented black Poodle who is mincing across the Park, complete with enormous mane and hair styling, with a minute waist and a very long tail carried at a jaunty perpendicular angle. He is quite in keeping with the military officer with his wildly exaggerated bearskin, and the ladies with their wasp waists who are the centerpiece of the drawing. The date is 1821.

Perhaps one of the best known paintings is "Behind the Scenes," by Ludwig Knaus (1880). This shows a screened off area behind the circus where the artists are resting between turns. The clown is sitting at the back, feeding the baby with a bottle, while the equestrienne (possible his wife) is resting with a wrap around her shoulders. There is a general air of untidiness, but the main point of interest in these circumstances is a group of two white Poodles and a black one, lying on the floor waiting for their act to be called.

Landseer painted a picture called "Laying Down the Law," in 1840, and in this a learned white Poodle is briefing dogs of other breeds. Toulouse-Lautrec also made many drawings of Poodles, mostly with a circus background. Many will have seen the fascinating drawings by Walter Crane, illustrating the children's nursery rhyme, "Old Mother Hubbard." These are most amusing, although the Poodle featured more resembles a bear, and the shortness of the ears would cause any Poodle breeder to shudder.

From the foregoing it will be seen that since the sixteenth century, artists have been attracted to the Poodle as a worthwhile subject, and he has certainly appeared in works of art as much as any other breed of dog. In these modern days, many beautiful photographs of Poodles have been taken, principally because as a breed they have a pronounced sense of vanity, and are always ready to pose for the photographer. White Poodles are particularly photogenic, and a great many really glorious examples of the Poodle have appeared in photographic exhibitions the world over, and they are constantly being featured in movies and on television.

American, Mexican and Canadian Champion La Petite Gai Dondi, handled by Mitch Wooten, and owned by Helen R. Agostinacci of South Gate, California.

III Poodle Personalities—Past and Present

Corded Poodles were first registered at the English Kennel Club as early as 1875, and the first Poodle champion was crowned in 1890. He was a large dog named "Achilles," owned by a Mr. Chance. Until 1904, Curly and Corded Poodles were registered as one variety, but that year saw the two types divided into separate varieties, and from then on the Corded Poodle slowly faded out. Miniature Poodles were first registered in England in 1910, and Toy Poodles were given recognition in 1957.

In England, Poodles reached their zenith in the years between 1950 and the present time. In 1954 Miniatures topped the registration totals and were to stay at the top for next ten years, until 1965 when they were superseded by Alsatians (German Shepherds). Toy Poodles ran very close to the Miniatures in second place during the years 1960-1963, but never succeeded in surpassing them numerically. In 1962 Miniature Poodles polled more than two and a half times the registrations of any other breed of dog, with a total of 20,102. But this was not their best year, for in 1960 they reached the figure of 23,216.

There is no doubt that during the years from 1950 to 1965, a tremendous number of really magnificent specimens were bred in England, and a great many of these found their way into the American Show Ring. But it is not always good for a breed to become so numerically superior, for, unfortunately, many inferior Poodles were also bred by those who did not care too much about the ultimate good of the breed, and some of these unworthy specimens found their way across the Atlantic.

Pioneer Breeders

But to return to the early part of this century, not a great deal of interest was then being shown in Poodles of any of the three sizes, although a few pioneers of the breed were hard at work evolving good specimens in both America and England, and these dogs gave much to the lovely Poodles seen in both countries today. Among the early breeders of Poodles in the States were Miss Alger, Mrs. Moulton, Mrs. Tyler-Morse, Mr. and Mrs. Hartman, Mrs. Flora Bonney; and in the English Poodle world such names as Miss Brunker (who incidentally was American by birth), Mrs. Graves, Mrs. Lee French, Miss Moorhouse and Mrs. Ionides were prominent. Progressing on to the 1920's, Miss Thorowgood, Mrs. Lowry, Mrs. D'Arcy Thompson (Rathnally), Miss Jane Lane (Nunsoe), Mrs. Murray Wilson (Stillington), Mr. and Mrs. Megroz (Colerne Down), Mrs. Boyd (Piperscroft), Mrs. May Pacey (Chaseley), Mrs. Tyndall (Vendas), Mrs. Campbell-Inglis (Mannerhead), Mrs. Hudson (Wigginton) and Mrs. Munro (Firebrave), are well known as careful breeders

The long ear fringes of a show Poodle are very important. Unfortunately, they are likely to become soiled with food and broken or worn. One method of protecting them is to wrap them in poleythylene as shown here. While still young he must be trained to ignore these appendages.

who had a great love for the Poodle, and did much to set the pattern for the beautiful sound structure of this breed in our time. Some of the outstanding dogs being shown at that time in England were Champion Cheeky Boy, Chatty, Chopstick, all of Chieveley; Whippendall's Boule de Neige, Dare Devil Dink; Champion Louis and Champion Barty of Piperscroft; Eric Brighteyes, Bonny Forget-me-not, Champion The Laird, Champion Flashlight, and Champion The Mistress, all of Mannerhead; Firebrave Cupidon, and Champion Firebrave Gaulois.

In the States, little had been heard of Poodles from the early days until the 1930's when Mrs. Whitehouse Walker of Bedford, New York, with several other enthusiastic breeders, founded the Poodle Club of America in 1931. Mrs. Slote at this time finished to champion her magnificent German-bred dog Donar V. Eisentor. And in 1934 the glorious Standard International Champion Nunsoe Duc de la Terrace of Blakeen, imported from England by Mrs. Sherman Hoyt, won Best in Show at the Westminster Show in Madison Square Garden.

The Brace Class waiting its turn to be judged. Larger shows, both in England and in America, frequently have "Brace" classes. The basis for judging this class is how well matched the two dogs are. The show points are not considered essential in the judging. However, how could the judge, being only human, fail to be swayed even a little by the quality of the dogs.

In 1933, Whippendell Poli won a Non-Sporting Group, and in 1935, Mrs. Milton Erlanger made up her first home-bred Champion in Cadeau de Noel; and Mrs. Sherman Hoyt's Blakeen Mary Mont finished, and also had the distinction of being the dam of five champions.

1934 saw the first American Miniature Champion in Marcourt Julia, and in 1937 Carillon Courage was the first Poodle to win a Non-Sporting Group and also an Obedience Trial at the same show. Mrs. Githens also finished her Carillon Corbeau, which was trained and handled in Obedience by the late Blanche Saunders. Mrs. Githens retired her Kennel in 1943 and handed over her Carillon prefix to Mrs. Saunders.

In 1940, Mr. and Mrs. George Putnam made up their first home-bred Champion in Puttencove Peachstone. This was the era of the owner handler in America, and it was not until much later that the professional handler, so well-known today, came on the scene.

International Champion Pixiecroft Krusader. In this picture, Krusader displays perfectly everything that a groomer can produce to enhance the beauty of a Poodle about to enter the ring. Top groomer and professional handler, Bernelle Hartman, spent about five hours achieving this result.

Poodle Clubs

Here are a few details of the various Clubs that are in existence for Poodles. The Poodle Club of America was founded in 1931 by Mrs. Whitehouse Walker and several enthusiastic breeders, and from then on many other Poodle Clubs were formed in various States, such Clubs mostly being affiliated with the Poodle Club of America.

In England, the original Poodle Club was founded in 1876 (though not formally adopted until 1896) and followed in 1932 by the International Poodle Club which was founded by Mrs. Campbell Inglis. The authors founded the South Western Poodle Club in 1950, which was the first of the regional Clubs, and this was quickly followed by the Trent to Tweed Poodle Club in 1952, the Midland Counties Poodle Club and the Poodle Club of Northern Ireland in 1955, and the Poodle Club of Scotland in 1957. The British Toy Poodle Club was inaugurated in 1956. All these Poodle Clubs hold an annual Championship Show where Challenge Certificates are on award, and also several smaller Open Shows and Members' Shows.

The English Kennel Club was founded in 1873 with the object of forming a code of rules governing the showing and breeding of dogs. Today this organization has reciprocal agreements with similar bodies in 36 different countries.

English Champion Adastra Magic Beau. In 1950 this blue Miniature Poodle, owned by Mr. and Mrs. L. H. C. Coventon, was awarded Supreme Best in Show at Cruft's, leading well over 5,000 dogs of all breeds. A few months later he won the Supreme Best in Show at Ayr Championship Show, followed by Best in Show at the International Poodle Club Show.

This adorable little Toy may never win a dog show, but she displays all the beauty and charm which has made the Poodle so popular all over the world

Dog Shows

Cruft's Show, held annually in February in England. is the largest show in the world. It was originated by Mr. Charles Cruft in 1886 at the old Aquarium in London, but moved to the Royal Agricultural Hall in Islington, London, in 1891, where it was held every year until 1938 when Charles Cruft died at the age of eighty-six. Then the English Kennel Club took over the management of the Show, and it was moved to Olympia, an exhibition hall in London. It has been held there every year with the exception of the World

War II years, and 1954 when the Show was cancelled at the eleventh hour because of a strike of electricians at Olympia.

The number of entries is colossal, and an all time record was achieved over two days in 1964 when 8,277 dogs made a total entry of 16,022. Dogs need be in the hall only on the day their breed is being judged. America's premier dog show, The Westminster, is also a two day affair. However, all dogs entered are required to be present both days.

As the number of entries increased year by year, space was becoming far too cramped even in the enormous building of Olympia. So in 1966, the minimum age for exhibiting puppies was raised from six months to eight months, and this certainly had some effect in controlling numbers. Exhibitors and spectators were upset at the disappearance from the ring of the really young show puppy of six months, but there was no alternative. In any case, numbers had still to be curtailed, and in 1967 the qualifying definition for entry at Cruft's stated that any dog or bitch must have gained a First, Second or Third prize in a breed class at a Championship Show at some time during the previous twelve months. This immediately eliminated inferior specimens and enhanced the quality tremendously, and also had the advantage of cutting the number of entries down to a manageable level. As a result, total entries at Cruft's in 1967 dropped to 12,302 as against 14,913 in 1966.

Several Poodles have been successful over the years in winning either the Supreme Best in Show at Cruft's or else the honor of Reserve Best in Show. In 1950, Mr. and Mrs. L. H. C. Conventon's blue Miniature, Champion Adastra Magic Beau, was awarded Supreme Best in Show, and so far no other Miniature has climbed so high at Cruft's. This wonderful dog was able to beat well over 5000 dogs of all breeds, and a few months later won the Supreme Best in Show at Ayr Championship Show, followed by Best in Show at the International Poodle Club Show.

Five years later, in 1955, Mrs. Proctor's brown Standard Poodle Champion Tzigane Aggri of Nashend, won the Supreme Award of Best in Show, the first time a Standard Poodle had achieved this honor. There were 91 entries made by 59 Standards, and Mrs. Barber was the breed judge. The total number of entries at Cruft's that year war 11.869, from 6,127 dogs.

Ten years on, in 1966, a lovely little apricot Toy Poodle, Champion Oakington Puckshill Ambersunblush, owned by Mr. and Mrs.

English Champion Tzigane Aggri of Nashend. In 1955 this outstanding brown Standard Poodle, owned by Mrs. Proctor, won the Supreme Best in Show at Cruft's, the first time a Standard Poodle had achieved this honor. The total number of entries at Cruft's that year was 11,869 from 6,127 dogs.

Paul Perry and bred by Mrs. Myles Dobson, was judged Supreme Best in Show. There were 242 Toy Poodles, making an entry of 405, while the overall entry was 14,913 from 7,773 dogs of all breeds, and Mr. Fred Cross was the judge for the Toy Poodle Bitches.

The next year, 1967, the well-known and glorious Standard Poodle International Champion, Bibelot's Tall, Dark and Handsome, won his breed class and his Group, and was judged Reserve Best in Show, just being beaten to top place by the Lakeland Terrier. Tall, Dark and Handsome is owned by Mrs. S. Fraser of Canada, and was most beautifully handled in the ring by Miss Marylyn Willis.

The Standard Poodle judge was again Mrs. Winnie Barber, and there were 63 Standards, making an entry of 99, while the overall entry was 12,302 from 6,845 dogs of all breeds. It was a tremendous disappointment to all Poodle enthusiasts that the fabulous Poodle was just passed at the post. However, he flew to the States from England the next day for the Westminster Show in New York, where with his devoted handler, Marylyn Willis, out of 25 Champions in the Special Class he made the final three. He also took Best of Breed at Detroit, and just after that he gained Best of Breed at the Poodle Club Specialty at the Sportsman Show in Toronto

This is American Champion Mike-Mar's Dream Come True, a male cafe-au-lait Toy Poodle. Mike is 2½ years old. While Mike is in show clip, his coat has been oiled with baby oil as protection. This will be bathed away when he is being readied for a show. Owned by Michael Wolf of Babylon, New York.

(only being beaten to Best in Show by Mr. Osborne's Tophill Orsino) – truly a magnificent Poodle of our time. His call name is "Tramp" and surely no Poodle has been so famous nor so well loved on both sides of the Atlantic.

Of the large American Shows, possibly the Westminster Show enjoys the most prestige, though it does not always draw the most entries. Occupying two days at the Madison Square Garden, it is a great social event as well as a canine one, and certainly the cream of America's Poodles can be seen there. The authors had the distinction of breeding the best brace of Toy Poodles (Champion Rothara the Little Snowflutter and Rothara the Little Toff) in 1965, when this event was won by Mrs. Maybelle Neuguth.

The Harbor Cities Show founded by the late Ernie Ferguson and Dave Upright in 1938, was considered one of the greatest American Shows, but was closed down at the death of Mr. Ferguson in 1964. That year, an entry of over 3600 had been received.

Another extremely important American Show is that of the International Kennel Club of Chicago, which in April of 1965 held its Silver Anniversary (25th) show, drawing an entry of 2986 dogs, and here the Poodles (of all three sizes) led the breeds with 195 entries.

A comparison of the relevant entries over a period of five years at both the Westminster Show in America and Cruft's Show in England may prove of interest here:

	Westminster			*Cruft's*		
Year	Stds	Mins	Toys	Stds	Mins	Toys
1963	34	77	85	116	566	485
1964	35	73	82	119	542	481
1965	31	84	68	84	459	373
1966	46	92	54	110	382	405
1967	54	54	56	99	384	303

It is hoped that the foregoing facts and figures may inspire the novice to join the ranks of the seasoned Poodle exhibitors, and perhaps add more honors to the credit of this fascinating and glamorous dog, the Poodle.

We talk about show dogs having outstanding heads, or outstanding angulation, or good proportions. However, in order to become an international champion like Pixiecroft Krusader, a dog must have not just one or two or three of these characteristics but all of them, and to a marked degree. In addition to the physical characteristics, he must have outstanding ring presence and showmanship. It took all of these, plus that intangible "something," for Krusader to become Champion in both Canada and the United States. International Champion Pixiecroft Krusader is owned by Pixiecroft Kennels in New York.

IV Show Points of the Poodle

We have looked into the past history of the Poodle, and have pointed out some statistics on this fascinating breed which indicate its present day popularity. The decision has been made – we hope – a Poodle is for you!

Whether you are paying a few dollars or several hundred, there are three points that you are entitled to insist upon when choosing your puppy, and if the puppy does not have these three essentials, our advice is to refuse to buy and to look elsewhere:

a) absolute cleanliness
b) good rearing
c) friendly temperament

These are within the scope of the careful and conscientious breeder, and puppies who do not measure up to them should never be offered for sale. If purchasers refuse to buy puppies who do not have these three essentials, Poodles will remain the charming and delightful breed that they now are.

Here are the official Standards of the Breed recognized by the American Kennel Club and the Kennel Club (England). We suggest that you compare the two, or even better, learn by heart the points of the perfect Poodle.

The American Standard of the Breed

General Appearance, Carriage and Condition - *That of a very active, intelligent and elegant looking dog, squarely built, well proportioned, moving soundly and carrying himself proudly. Properly clipped in the traditional fashion and carefully groomed, the Poodle has about him an air of distinction and dignity peculiar to himself.*

Head and Expression – *(a) Skull: moderately rounded, with a slight but definite stop. Cheek-bones and muscles flat. Muzzle: long, straight and fine, with slight chiseling under the eyes. Strong without lippiness. The chin definite enough to preclude snipiness. Teeth white, strong and with a scissors bite. Nose sharp with well-defined nostrils. (b) Eyes: set far apart, very dark, full of fire and intelligence, oval in appearance. (c) Ears: set low and hanging close to the head. The leather should be long, wide and heavily feathered.*

Neck and Shoulders – *Neck well proportioned, strong and long to*

admit of the head being carried high and with dignity. Skin snug at throat. The neck should rise from strong muscular shoulders which slope back from their point of angulation at the upper foreleg to the withers.
Body – *The chest deep and moderately wide. The ribs well sprung and braced up. The short, strong and slightly hollowed, the loins short, broad and muscular. (Bitches may be slightly longer in back than dogs).*
Tail – *Straight, set on rather high, docked, but of sufficient length to insure a balanced outline. It should be carried up and in a gay manner.*
Legs – *The forelegs straight from the shoulder, parallel and with bone and muscle in proportion to size of dog. The pasterns should be strong. The hind legs very muscular, stifles well bent and hocks well let down. The thigh should be well developed, muscular and showing width in the region of the stifle to insure strong and graceful action. The four feet should turn neither in nor out.*
Feet – *Rather small and oval in shape. Toes arched, close and cushioned on thick, hard pads.*

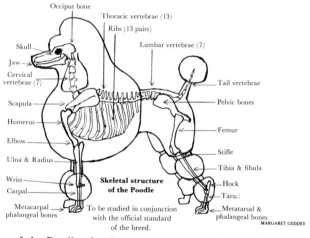

Occiput bone

Thoracic vertebrae (13)

Ribs (13 pairs)

Skull

Lumbar vertebrae (7)

Jaw

Cervical vertebrae (7)

Tail vertebrae

Scapula

Pelvic bones

Homerus

Femur

Elbow

Stifle

Ulna & Radius

Tibia & fibula

Wrist

Skeletal structure of the Poodle

Hock

Carpal

Tarsal

Metacarpal phalangeal bones

To be studied in conjunction with the official standard of the breed.

Metatarsal & phalangeal bones

MARGARET GEDDES

The skeleton of the Poodle, showing correct posture and bone formation.

Coat – *Quality: very profuse, of harsh texture and dense throughout.*
Clip – *A Poodle may be shown in the "Puppy" Clip, or in the traditional "Continental" Clip or the "English Saddle" Clip. A Poodle under a year old may be shown in the "Puppy" Clip with the coat long except the face, feet and base of tail. which should be shaved. Dogs one year old or older must be shown in either the "Continental" Clip or "English Saddle" Clip.*

Eve De Gillen being shown at ten months of age in a puppy clip. This clip is permissible for a show dog until he is one year old. Eve, a charming black Toy, has eleven points and needs a Major to complete her championship. Owner, Michael Gillen of New York.

In the "Continental" Clip the hindquarters are shaved with pom-pons on hips optional). The face, feet, legs and tail are shaved, leaving bracelets on the hind legs, puffs on the forelegs and a pompom at the end of the tail. The rest of the body must be left in full coat.

In the "English Saddle" Clip, the hindquarters are covered with a short blanket of hair except for a curved shaved area on the flank and two shaved bands on each hind leg. The face, feet, forelegs and tail are shaved leaving puffs on the forelegs and a pompon at the end of the tail. The rest of the body must be left in full coat.

Color – *The coat must be an even and solid color at the skin. In blues, grays, silvers, browns, cafe-au-laits, apricots and creams the coats may show varying shades of the same color. This is frequently present in the somewhat darker feathering of the ears and in the tipping of the ruff. While clear colors are definitely preferred, such natural variation in the shading of the coat is not to be considered a fault. Brown and cafe-au-lait Poodles have liver-colored noses, eye-rims and lips, dark toenails and dark amber eyes. Black, blue, gray, silver, apricot, cream and white Poodles have black noses, eye-rims and lips, black or self-colored toenails and very dark eyes. In the apricots, while black is preferred, liver-colored noses, eye-rims and lips, self-colored toenails and amber eyes are permitted but are not desirable.*

Gait – *A straightforward trot with light springy action. Head and tail carried high. Forelegs and hind legs should move parallel turning neither in nor out. Sound movement is essential.*

Size:

Standard – *The Standard Poodle is over 15 inches at the withers. Any Poodle which is 15 inches or less in height shall be disqualified from competition as a Standard Poodle.*

Miniature – *The Miniature Poodle is 15 inches or under at the withers, with a minimum height in excess of 10 inches. Any Poodle which is over 15 inches, or 10 inches or less at the withers shall be disqualified from competition as a Miniature Poodle.*

Toys – *The Toy Poodle is 10 inches or under at the withers. Any Poodle which is more than 10 inches at the withers shall be disqualified from competition as a Toy Poodle.*

Value of Points

General appearance, carriage and condition	*20*
Head, ears, eyes and expression	*20*
Neck and Shoulders	*10*
Body and tail	*15*
Legs and feet	*15*
Coat-color and texture	*10*
Gait	*10*
Total	*100*

A dog's height is always measured from the highest point of the shoulders to the ground. A shows how a hook measure is used, and B shows a "hound measure." In America, all Poodles are registered as "Poodle." There is no differentiation for size. This is done because a dog does not reach his full growth until he is one year of age, and a dog of Mini parents might be undersized and remain "Toy," or a puppy of Toy parentage may outgrow the Toy classification. Likewise with the difference between Miniature and Standard.

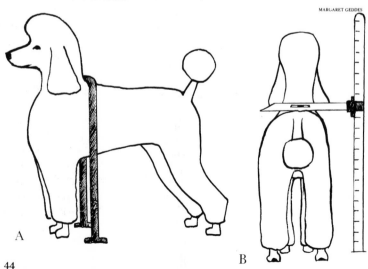

MARGARET GEDDES

A   B

Major Faults

Eyes: *round in appearance, protruding, large or very light. Jaws: undershot, overshot or wry mouth. Cowhocks. Feet: flat or spread.* **Tail:** *set low, curled or carried over the back. Shyness.*

Disqualifications

Parti-colors: *the coat of a parti-colored dog is not an even solid color at the skin but is variegated in patches of two or more colors.*
Any type of clip other than those listed in section on coat.
Any size over or under the limits specified in section on size.

Approved July 14, 1959

(Reprinted by kind permission of the American Kennel Club).
As will have been seen, the standard of the breed lays down precisely the points of the perfect Poodle. The English standard is very similar, differing only slightly in one or two minor points. However, it may be interesting to compare the two standards.

The Official Standard Of the Breed - English (Standard Poodle)

General Appearance. *That of a very active, intelligent, and elegant-looking dog, well built, and carrying himself very proudly.*
Head and Skull. *Head long and straight and fine, the skull not broad, with a slight peak at the back. Muzzle long (but not snipy) and strong – not full in cheek, lips black and not showing lippiness. Nose black and sharp.*
Eyes. *Almond-shaped, very dark, full of fire and intelligence.*
Ears. *The leather long and wide, low set on, hanging close to the face.*
Mouth. *Teeth white, strong and level.*
Neck. *Well-proportioned and strong, to admit of the head being carried high and with dignity.*
Forequarters. *Shoulders strong and muscular, sloping well to the back. Legs set straight from shoulder, with plenty of bone and muscle.*
Body. *Chest deep and moderately wide. Back short, strong, and slightly hollowed, the loins broad and muscular, the ribs well sprung and braced up.*
Hindquarters. *Legs very muscular and bent, with the hocks well let down.*

A magnificently headed white Standard Poodle showing the almond-shaped eyes, narrow skull, and black pigmentation of eye rims, lips and nose.

A white Miniature Poodle in Dutch Clip. The hair is clipped short on face, feet and tail, and around the body, while on fore- and hindlegs it is left quite long, with somewhat exaggerated pads on shoulders and hips. In this example, the Poodle is still left with quite a full beard. Although in companion clip, his stance is that of a show dog.

An apricot Toy (English) of excellent deep color, profuse coat, and well-shaped hindquarters. The expression is alert, with dark eyes and good nose pigment.

Feet. *Rather small and of good shape, the toes well arched, pads thick and hard.*

Tail. *Set on rather high, well carried, never curled or carried over the back.*

Coat. *Very profuse and of good hard texture; if corded, hanging in tight, even cords; if non-corded, very thick and strong of even length, the curls close and thick without knots or cords. It is strongly recommended that the traditional Lion Clip should be adhered to.*

Color. *All black, all white, all brown, all blue and all solid colors. The white Poodle should have dark eyes, black nose, lips, and toe-nails. The brown Poodle should have dark amber eyes, dark liver nose, lips be of even color, and have dark eyes, lips and toe-nails. All the other points of white, brown, and blue Poodles should be the same as the perfect black Poodle.*

Weight and Size. *15 inches and over.*

Poodle (Miniature)

The Miniature Poodle should be in every respect a replica, in miniature, of the Standard Poodle. Height at shoulder must be under 15 inches.

Faults. *In the Miniature Poodle: heavy build, clumsiness, long back, light, round and prominent eyes, bad stern carriage, heavy gait, coarse head, over or undershot mouth, flesh-colored nose, coarse legs and feet, open and rusty coats, white markings on black and colored Poodles, or other markings on white Poodles.*

Poodle (Toy)

The standard of the Poodle (Toy) is the same as that of the Poodle (Standard) and Poodle (Miniature) except that the height at shoulder must be under 11 inches.

(Reprinted by kind permission of English Kennel Club).

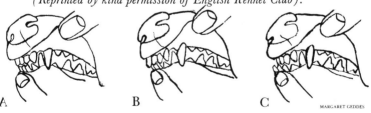

Teeth formation. A: Pincer bite, B: Scissor bite, and C: Incorrect undershot teeth.

The Companion Poodle

If you want a Poodle for a pet or companion only, you may have to accept one which has, undoubtedly, some show flaws in order to get him at the price you can afford. You cannot expect to get the perfect or even near perfect Poodle at a pet dog price. Here are a few common faults which may be found in the Poodle that would preclude his winning in the show ring but do not affect his value as a first class companion.

First, the mouth should be level, that is the front teeth, both upper and lower, should meet evenly together in what is called a "pincer bite", or equally, the top set may fit tightly over the lower set in what is known as a "scissor bite," and either of these are correct. But if the lower front teeth protrude beyond the top teeth, it is known as being "undershot" – the *under* jaw *shooting* out beyond the upper jaw. If the top front teeth protrude over the bottom teeth to any extent, it is referred to as being "overshot," and is still a fault though preferable to undershot. An undershot dog has an aggressive and pugilistic expression, while an overshot dog looks mean and snipy. These distinctions can be readily seen in the accompanying diagram. Quite often the correct number of teeth are not present, deficiencies being most usual either in the premolars or in the small front teeth. Equally, and this happens quite often with the Toy Poodle, the mouth may be just too small to accommodate the full number of teeth evenly, and consequently these teeth are crowded and jumbled – all not too serious faults in the pet, but not to be tolerated in the show dog.

Tail set may not be all that could be desired, for the tail may curl too much over the puppy's back, or it may be a little low set. If so, he will have difficulty in raising it perpendicularly as he should.

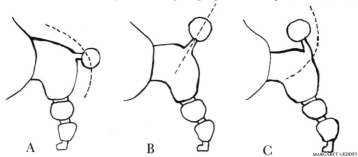

MARGARET GEDDES

Tail set. A: Low set, carrying with it roach back and straight stifle. B: Correct carriage. C: Squirrel or gay tail, caused by swayback.

MARGARET GEDDES

Eye formation. A: Correct; almond-shaped eye. B: Incorrect; too large and round.

Pigmentation in the light-colored Poodle is another fault that may be evident. In a white or apricot show Poodle, jet black nose, lips and eye rims are desirable, but in a pet Poodle, brownish or not so black pigmentation might be tolerated.

A large, round eye is not considered correct, although this often gives the companion Poodle a glamorous and "pretty" expression. The correct eye should be almond-shaped, dark and full of fire.

All the foregoing, while faults in a show specimen, make little difference to the Poodle himself whose main function in these circumstances is to be a loving and devoted companion to his owner.

If it is a show specimen you have in mind, you must study the standard of the breed most carefully, and try to recognize in the puppy you are considering the various attributes and faults that he may have in his make-up. You cannot expect to purchase a completely perfect dog with nothing wrong. Some faults have a reasonable chance of either being rectified or, at any rate, of improving with maturity, and others are so slight as to be worth taking a chance on since the good points may well outweigh the doubtful ones. Some faults you will see at a glance are severe and are not to be tolerated at all.

You can only understand the difference between good and bad points by studying winning dogs whenever possible, and by studying the breed standard frequently and carefully.

To help you in the choice of a good quality show puppy, we shall now consider the Poodle standard in detail, pointing out some of the dangerous pitfalls, and helping you to observe the differences between good and bad in structure and conformation.

You will wish first to examine the mouth, and so you must know about teeth formation. Puppies cut their baby teeth between four and seven weeks old and usually suffer little reaction, but the second and adult teeth come through between 14 weeks and seven months, and may cause trouble. Often the puppy's gums are red and fiery, and his mouth painful to the touch. As a result, during this time he is difficult to clip, may go off his food, may suffer from frequent bouts of mild digestive trouble, and may become a little unreliable in his house cleanliness.

At the worst, he may indulge in teething fits or convulsions, but this is not usual. When the second teeth are all safely through, there should be 44 in all. There should be in both upper and lower jaws six incisors (small front teeth) which are sub-divided into "nippers" which are the two middle teeth, "intermediates" which are those on either side of the nippers, and "corners" which come next. Then there is one large "canine" on either side of the six small teeth. Behind these come the "pre-molars" and the "molars" of which there are usually seven on each side of both upper and lower jaws, making a total of 44. When purchasing a dog of an age to have formed all his teeth, the number and correct placement should always be verified. The incisors and canines can be seen in a young puppy, but the molars and pre-molars may not be through until six months of age or even older.

A fault may often be detected in the number of puppy teeth, for there may be only four incisors in either top or bottom jaw. It is unlikely, though not impossible, that in this case there will be the correct number of six in the adult teeth. The muzzle itself should be long and strong, with a certain amount of chin, and the cheeks should be flat with no heavy bone on either side of the forehead.

There should be a certain amount of chiseling under the eyes. Faults here are a falling away under the jaw with little or no chin, giving a snipy, mean expression, or else rather heavy and pendulous lips resembling a Spaniel. There should be chunky heavy bone at the top of the cheek. The nose should be black and well defined. A "dudley" or "butterfly" nose (pink with black spots) is a fault. The nose in a light colored puppy will usually turn grey at about

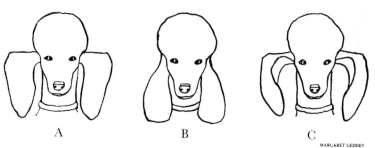

A   B   C

Ear carriage. A: High set ears hanging at right angles to the face. B: Correct ear set, with leathers hanging close to head. C: Flying ears, which are incorrect and often seen in puppies when teething. This condition will usually correct itself.

three days of age and should be jet black by the time he is four to eight weeks of age. If the nose is still pink or spotted at eight weeks, it is very suspect and not likely to turn completely black as it should. Dark colored puppies are born with black noses, and brown Poodles with brown noses,

The eyes of the Poodle are one of his beauties. They should be dark, full of fire and intelligence. They should also have a "kind" expression, and there should be nothing mean or crafty in them. They should be almond shaped and not too large. The full round glamorous eye has already been discussed; it is a fault, although it adds a cute expression to the pet Poodle.

The skull should be fine with a slight top between the eyes. There should be quite a pronounced occiput bone which is a boney protruberance at the rear of the skull. A round "apple head" is a fault.

Next come the ears which must be low set and hang close to the head. The leathers should be wide, long, and with long fringing on the end which should grow to several inches when the puppy is almost adult. Common faults are high set ears, ears which are inclined to hang at right angles to the face, and those which do not hang close to the head. A well-set ear orifice should be positioned just below a horizontal line drawn from the eye. Puppies quite often "fly" their ears during both first and second teething, but these right themselves as the condition passes.

The neck should be moderately long to allow the head to be carried high and with elegance. A short neck, often referred to as "ewe" neck, takes all the style from a Poodle, while a too long thin neck ("swan neck") is equally ugly. There should be no sagging skin at the throat.

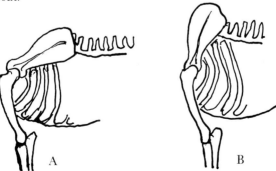

Shoulder formation. A: Shoulder sloping backward, causing correct front angulation in foreleg. B: Straight shoulder blade, causing stiff gait.

Shoulders must be strong and muscular, and slope backwards to cause good angulation. The diagram will show this point. A Poodle with a straight shoulder, giving no angulation, will have impeded motive power and a short step, so that he will miss out on the typical dancing action, and will not cover the ground strongly as he should.

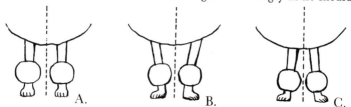

A: Correct foreleg positioning. B: Incorrect, the chest too wide and the toes are turned out. C: Incorrect, chest too narrow, the feet turn out.

The front legs should fall in two parallel lines from the shoulder, with the feet and toes facing strictly to the front, and with no tendency to turning either inwards or outwards. The drawing shows faults in foreleg structure resulting from a too wide chest, with ankles turning inwards and feet turning outwards, giving what is known as the "Queen Anne" look (referring to the style of furniture designed in England during the reign of Queen Anne, where the legs are bowed and the feet turn outwards). A Poodle's feet should be small and elegant, with strongly tensioned muscles in the toes, and close, thick and cushioned pads. A wide, long foot is not desirable, nor one that is flabby, giving the impression of being webbed.

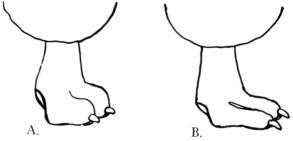

MARGARET GEDDES

Feet. A: Correct, well-muscled toes and thick pads. B: A long, flabby foot. This is undesirable.

A short back is desirable in a male Poodle, though the female may advantageously have an extra inch to facilitate her breeding propensities. The back should be just slightly hollowed, though not by any means pendulous enough to justify the expression "sway-backed". Equally, a hunched back, or "roach back" is a bad fault, as this causes the head to poke forward and the tail to be low set and drooping. The drawing illustrates the correctly balanced Poodle, and shows that it should be possible to draw an imaginary perpendicular line from the top of the head, down over the ear, over the side of the shoulder and straight down the foreleg to the ground, another line from the top of the tail, down over the thigh to the floor, with the lower part of the hind leg and the hock stretching out beyond and to the back of this line.

A well-proportioned Poodle puppy should give the impression of being square and chunky, and the measurement from the base of the neck to the root of the tail should equal the measurement from the top of the shoulder to the ground. The Poodle body profile thus represents a square.

The Poodle's rib cage must be well-rounded; this is known as a good "spring of rib", while the reverse is referred to as being "shelly," that is, flat sided with little roundness or strength. The loins should be strong and powerful, with well-covered thighs.

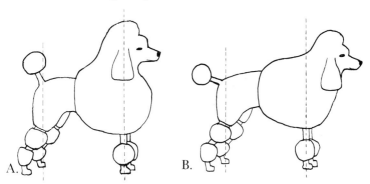

MARGARET GEDDES

Poodle balance. This term is vague, yet "balance" is what every Poodle judge looks for. Roughly defined, it would include posture, alertness, proportions and an overall Poodle look. A shows the correct, upstanding conformation. B is ill-balanced; the head is poking forward, the back is roached, and the tail set too low.

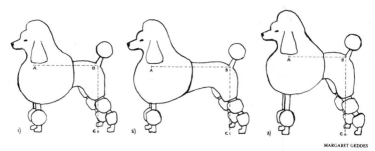

MARGARET GEDDES

Poodle proportions. 1) This is a correctly proportioned Poodle; the lines from A to B and from B to C are of equal length. 2) This dog is too long for his height. 3) This dog is too "leggy."

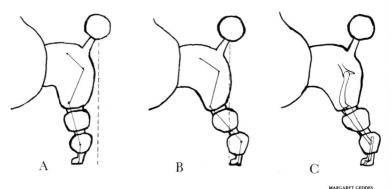

MARGARET GEDDES

Hind leg formation. A: This is undesirable. There is not enough angulation, and the stifle is straight with the hind legs pinned in. B: The angulation is correct. The hocks extend beyond a dotted line drawn form the tail perpendicular to the ground. C: Shows the underlying bone formation necessary for correct angulation at haunch, stifle and hock.

The hind legs of the Poodle are all important, for they supply the dog's motive power. Therefore, there must be plenty of muscle, and above all, good angulation. From the diagram it will be seen that the bone structure must follow a zig-zag pattern, and both the first and the second thigh (that is, above and below the stifle joint) must be particularly well muscled, going down to the hocks which should be "well let down," meaning near to the ground within moderation, and well stretched back.

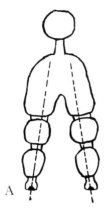
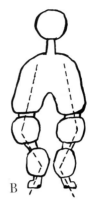

As viewed from the rear, A is correct. B is incorrect; the dog is cow-hocked and the toes are turned out.

The dog that has a straight stifle where there is little angulation in the bone structure, will be "pinned in" with a stiff and stilted gait, and he will not be able to cover the ground as he should. So check on that angulation – it is so very important. It is quite possible to determine whether the young puppy is free in the hindquarters by making two quite simple tests. The puppy may be lifted and held up by placing the left hand between his front legs and under the chest, with the right hand holding him up by his tail. This is naturally an uncomfortable position for the puppy and he should only be held for a second or so. The puppy's front legs and back legs should fall in a straight downward line from the shoulders and haunch respectively. If the hind legs incline towards the front, he may well be "pinned in". If he kicks his legs out backward, this is an excellent sign.

The second test is to stand the puppy on a steady, level surface, and lift his hindquarters up by his tail for an inch or so and then let his tail go, when his feet will return to their normal position. If the feet are moderately stretched out behind beyond his rump, this is good, but if they swing in towards his front legs this is not a favorable sign.

Another test for correct leg formation is to put one hand through the back legs and on to the belly, at the same time draw the hind legs out backward. If both hind legs stretch backward easily, there is obviously excellent angulation which will lead to correct gait,

Mike-Mar's Ebony, a chocolate Toy, is champion sired. Now 3 years old and shown here in show clip, he is kept as a pet by Mrs. Eugene Dann of New York. Many owners of otherwise fine dogs never bother to show them, preferring to keep them solely as much-loved family pets.

but if the hindquarters seem difficult to pull back and cause slight discomfort to the puppy. this can only mean that the bones are too straitly cushioned into the joint sockets and have little power to move freely as they should.

To test for straight front legs. lift the puppy's front end up for a couple of inches by placing a hand on either side of his shoulders or neck. and then drop him gently back on his feet. The two legs should fall in an absolutely parallel vertical line. By this means it is easy to see if the legs run inwards at the toes, or vice versa.

A lot of time has been spent in discussing the angulation and the soundness of the legs, but this angulation is of paramount importance. and on it depends the entire posture and gait that is so typical of the well-formed show Poodle.

Next examine the tail. This is another important part of the Poodle. for it really gives an indication of this temperament as well as indicating that his conformation is correct. The desired angle of the tail should either be completely upright or else inclining very slightly away from the body. Think of a clock – the correct tail position is either twelve o'clock or five minutes past one. A tail that is carried down in the twenty minutes past four position is a sorry sight, giving the Poodle a dreary and depressed expression. This position is usually the result of a roach back, which carries with it the poking head and low set tail.

But equally, a gay or "squirrel" tail, one that is carried over the back at the position of ten minutes to ten or even fifteen minutes to nine, gives the Poodle a raffish and common look, and undoubtedly destroys his elegance and dignity. It is the result of a sway-back which carries with it the too-high set tail. This also affects front leg action, as the head will be thrown too far back, causing the Poodle to prance excessively with front legs plaiting or weaving.

So the ideal tail set is seen when the tail is set on to the end of a straight backbone, and carried as vertically as possible. This again is quite simple to check in a puppy.

The coat of the Poodle is a thing of great beauty. Certainly it can be selectively bred because many strains of Poodles both in America and England are famous for their profuse and luxuriant coats. The texture must be strong and springy, with the curls close and dense. The shorter hair of the Poodle should curl strongly, but where the hair grows long it will be somewhat straighter, for the weight of the hair pulls out the ends.

Thus, the Poodle in Lamb Clip or Dutch Clip has a coat which is far more curly than the dog which is kept in the traditional Lion Clip, where the mane is many inches long. Density of coat is correct, and when you blow on it, the hair should not part; in fact, it should be quite difficult to get down to the skin of the true textured coat. A thin coat, or a very soft coat, is a fault as is one which is "felty" or inclined to resemble cotton wool.

A good test in an adult dog is to press down on the coat with your hand. The hair should feel thick and resistant, and when your hand is removed, the coat should spring back into position and show no sign of having been pressed upon. The puppy which has a profuse thick coat is generally all set for the correct bushy adult coat. But the thin, soft and rather wispy coat has not much chance of developing later on in maturity.

A puppy may remain in puppy clip (that is, with the coat left long on his body, with just the face, feet and tail clipped close) until he is a year old, after which time he must – if shown – appear either in the English saddle clip or the continental lion clip. Equally, he may be put into either of these two styles before he is a year old or the puppy clip, if desired. But these are the only three clipping styles admissable in the American show ring.

Though there is quite a deal of latitude regarding the color of Poodles. only solid self colors are permitted. A parti-colored Poodle, popularly called a phantom, is disqualified for show purposes. A certain amount of shading is tolerated, for often the final self color takes some time to develop, and the color of the hair at the roots may be somewhat lighter than the top ends of the coat, particularly in blues, greys, silvers, browns and apricots. This darker hair is particularly noticeable on the ends of the ear fringes, and on the tipping of the mane. While not actually considered a fault, a dog whose coat has completely cleared will take precedence, all other points equal, over the Poodle who still has obvious darker shading.

In America, there is considerable agitation for the acceptance of the bicolored Poodle but so far this has fallen on deaf ears of those in authority. Some of the bicolored dogs are very beautiful.

The sizes of the three varieties of Poodles have already been mentioned, but it must be repeated that for the show ring the Standard Poodle must exceed fifteen inches at the withers, or shoulders, while the Miniature Poodle must measure fifteen inches or under, at the withers, but must not measure as little as ten inches or less. The Toy Poodle must measure ten inches or less at the shoulder, although in England and many other countries the Toy Poodle is allowed another inch, giving him a top height of eleven inches. But there are many classes scheduled in the English show ring for Toy Poodles of ten inches or less.

We have tried to show you the desired show points of the Poodle compared with the undesirable ones, but of course these characteristics may not all have developed or be apparent in the eight to twelve week old puppy. It is quite possible that you will have to take your chances with some of them, hoping that they develop correctly as the Poodle matures. But many points *will* be manifest in the young puppy, particularly the structural ones like the well-laid back shoulder, the correctly angulated hindquarters, and the well set-on tail, and also the short, cobby back. Bracing-up of ribs, fineness of skull, and length of muzzle may not be too evident, but should develop as the puppy matures.

Above all, the matter of balance must be studied, for herein lies the key to Poodle elegance. A long backed Poodle on short legs is a dreadful sight, for he is unquestionably clumsy and inelegant, and his gait is ugly as he stumps along with heavy tread. This is not a desirable Poodle! A good Poodle should have the action almost of

This is a champion black Miniature Poodle in the correct show stance, with head held erect and in a perpendicular line with the front legs. The tail is at the correct angle and the hindquarters show excellent angulation.

the ballet dancer – a light and dancing movement full of agility, grace and beauty. Equally, the Poodle who is too short in the back and too long in the leg presents a comic picture, for instead of the delightful dancing action, he walks as though he were on stilts, with a definite mincing movement.

Monorchid or Cryptorchid

Another important point to be verified in a male dog is that he should be "entire," and by that is meant that he should have two testicles descended into the scrotum, otherwise he will not be eligible for the show ring. If only one testicle is descended, the dog is known as a monorchid, and while such dogs are able to sire puppies, they are not completely reliable, and so may "miss" with a female, and the litters sired may not be large. A dog that has no descended testicles is referred to as a cryptorchid, and in this state he is unable to sire puppies since he is completely sterile.

All male dogs exported to America and other countries from England must undergo an examination by a veterinarian, to certify that the testicles are fully descended, and a certificate must be sent to the English Kennel Club before the necessary export pedigree will be issued. In puppies, unlike those in boys, the testicles are descended

What could be more beautiful?

at birth. They may be felt manually from then onwards, but sometimes they are almost indiscernible before about 12 to 14 weeks.

If neither of the testicles, or if only one, can be definitely found on examination, the English exporter must notify the intending purchaser of this defect, and only if the purchaser sends a letter to the English Kennel Club to the effect that he understands the puppy is not completely entire, but that he still wants to purchase it, will the necessary export permit be issued.

It is equally important, in view of the rules for showing, and also because the dog may be wanted for mating later on, that the question of entirety be checked at the time of purchase. To make the examination, the puppy should be held on his back, belly up. Then the first two fingers of the hand should be passed *very gently* over the portion of skin just below the penis towards the groin in between the back legs. The two testicles will usually be discovered by this means, and will resemble two very small jellified lumps which move slightly as the fingers massage the flesh. Sometimes these two minute lumps can be detected quite easily soon after birth, although it is usually difficult until the puppy is at least eight weeks old.

If there is no trace of either or both testicles by the time the puppy is eight to ten months old, the outlook is doubtful. Again, the testicles have a habit of coming and going when the puppy is cutting his second teeth, one day being apparent, and the next, completely absent. But this is not usually serious, and all will be well when teething is completed.

If you do not feel competent to carry out this examination on the puppy you are about to purchase, a veterinarian will speedily do it for you.

It is hoped that this explanation of some of the points of the Poodle as laid down in the standards of the breed may help the prospective Poodle buyer to pick a worthy representative of the breed. It is not easy to differentiate between many of the good or bad points, but it is a knowledge which improves with practice, and the best way to become really selective is to attend Poodle shows and study the winning dogs, and, if possible, talk with owners and handlers about their dogs.

Study the diagrams carefully and regularly. While the faults depicted here are intentionally a little exaggerated, they should help you to recognize what you want and what you must have in a really good Poodle, either puppy or adult.

Oodles of Poodles! Which apricot shall we choose? They're all so lovable.

V Choosing the Puppy

You have now studied the correct standard of the Poodle, and should know what to look for. But there are still more decisions to be made. First, do you plan on a male or a female Poodle?

Male or Female

Both have their advantages; it is simply a matter of deciding which fits in with your personal circumstances.

Male dogs are a little more aggressive and may be slightly inclined to wander from home if given the opportunity, while females are not as interested in taking off, and are perhaps somewhat more placid than males. On the other hand, males are extremely devoted companions, inclined to attach themselves to one particular person rather than to all and sundry. Male dogs are well nigh tireless and always ready for a long walk, a race along the beach, or an energetic game with a ball.

Females are equally ready for anything, but they are also perhaps a little quieter in temperament. So possibly the choice rests more on your own feeling than anything else. There is the matter of a female coming into heat every six months which may present a problem, and influence your choice. Depending on the rapidity of growth, she will have her first heat from between six and fourteen months. Usually the large Standard Poodles commence their first season early, possibly about six to eight months, while the tiny Toy Poodles may not reach maturity until considerably later, possibly not before fourteen months.

Every six or seven months thereafter, normally the female will be in heat for approximately 17 to 21 days, and during that time she must be carefully segregated from male dogs, especially between the eighth and fifteenth days or she will try to find herself a mate. Obviously, this period of segregation can present problems, especially if you want your Poodle to accompany you to work, or plan to take her with you on frequent vacations. It may also present problems if you have young children, for one cannot expect youngsters always to remember to shut that gate, or lock that door. On the other hand, you may live somewhere away from other people and other dogs, and this twice yearly period of your female may not trouble you at all.

Best of all, you may plan to breed Poodles and so the decision is easy. However, one word of advice – unless you plan to run a kennel or have some experience of breedings dogs, it is not advisable to have both male and female in the same house or apartment. It is not fair to the male, and as you will not want to breed puppies every six months, accidents are bound to happen. So, if you plan to have more than one Poodle, keep to the same sex unless you have facilities to segregate them at these special times.

Of course, those who plan to keep their females solely as pets can have them spayed (altered). Done under anesthesia this constitutes a minimum of discomfort to the dog, and does not affect her temperament or personality. This removal of the ovaries prevents the female from ever going into "heat." As she is only sexually attractive to males during the heat period, and as this period is the only time the female is willing or capable of being mated, the operation eliminates this twice a year nuisance.

Black, white, apricot, or any other color, you can choose the color that satisfies you aesthetically. Under the coat all Poodles are friendly, loveable, adorable and loads of fun.

SALLY ANNE THOMPSON

What Color?

Another point is to be considered – color. In these days, there are a variety of lovely colors to choose from. In the old days, there were only three basics, black, white and brown. Then silver-grey was added, followed by blue, apricot, champagne, lavender, cafe-au-lait, parchment, and many others.

Oddly enough, each color seems to carry with it individual quirks of temperament, and again it is a matter of personal preference. Blacks and browns tend to be particularly lively, always up to some sort of devilment; the whites are placid, dignified and full of sagacity; the silver-greys are not particularly gregarious, rather seeming to prefer one person, and are a little possessive in their devotion. The most recent innovations in color, such as apricot, cafe-au-lait and others, have not yet developed any linked color temperament characteristics. This has been my personal experience; others may differ from me.

If you plan to breed Poodles, color may be important. Fashions come and go, and for several years one color may be a great favorite, and then, after a time lose its place to be superseded by another. Black, brown and white Poodles more often breed most true to their own color, and if their parents are of the same color, there is little danger of parti-color appearing in the litters. Silvers are born black; the silver may not appear until the puppies are several months old. Usually when first clipped, the face, feet and tail where the hair is clipped short, show the desired grey color, but the rest of the coat is shiny black. The grey comes in at the roots, and if the hair is parted, the silver can be detected, but a silver Poodle may take a long time, even years, before its color has completely cleared. This can be a drawback when selling the puppies. Apricots can be a glorious color but only those that are a really deep tan when young will remain a good apricot when grown. Those puppies who appear a lovely peachy-apricot at eight weeks or so will, most likely, fade to a dirty cream with tan ears when fully mature. Therefore, choose a really very dark tan puppy if you want an apricot of the correct rich color later.

Your Way of Life

When contemplating a new dog, choose one that will fit in with your own way of living. If you have a lot of spare time and are almost always home during the day, a young puppy will be right for you. But if you are away much of the time, and the pup will have to be left alone, it may be inconvenient to keep a young puppy. An older dog might be better able to cope with the situation. Moreover, if you are a traveller, circumstances may take you out of town far too often to even think of keeping a dog at all, unless you have someone to care for it during your absences.

There is another situation when a dog may prove something of a problem, and that is with newlyweds. It is likely that after a year of marriage the first baby may be on the way, and the young mother might have to divide her free time between the dog and the baby. If she is a real dog lover and highly motivated this can easily be done, but she should realize that it will require effort on her part. So it really is very important to decide beforehand if your circumstances really warrant the purchase of a puppy. For there is no doubt that you will have to make a few sacrifices, and deny yourself some pleasures.

Registration Papers

Now, if you have chosen a Poodle as your personal dog, you will want one that is purebred, and representative of the breed. Probably of all dogs, the crossbred Poodle is the easiest to "fake". Almost any longhaired puppy can be made to resemble a Poodle by judicious clipping. So be quite sure that the Poodle puppy you buy has the correct papers. After all, you are to have this puppy for the rest of its life, and it will be embarrassing and depressing if your friends continually ask, "What is it?" So be sure you have its papers and then you can be justifiably proud.

American Kennel Club Registration

When buying a purebred dog, the seller should give you registration papers made out to you in your name at the time the sale is made. If these are not yet available – as may very well happen because of red tape and regulations – the dealer must, at the barest minimum, give you in writing the name and registration number of the sire and dam of your puppy, the date of birth, and the name of the breeder. If he cannot provide these, you may very well question the authenticity of your puppy's registration.

In addition, the seller should guarantee in writing that he will provide papers for your puppy. These may not seem very important to you at the time of purchase, but you will see later on just how important they can be. Far too many people neglect to secure papers, feeling that they are important only for those people who intend to breed or show their dogs. And then when the puppy grows up to be a real beauty they regret overlooking the papers, because a dog not properly registered with the American Kennel Club cannot be entered in an American Kennel Club licensed show.

Unless *both* parents are registered, their offspring cannot be registered with the American Kennel Club. Should you fail to register your dog or should you mate it with an unregistered dog none of its puppies will be eligible for registration.

This 1 year old show bred Poodle, shown here in Royal Dutch clip, is not eligible for show because he is parti-colored. White markings can show up in any litter, but this does not affect their value as a pet. Candice of Hewlett Neck is being held by her owner's wife, Mrs. M. Certleman, of New York.

Also bear in mind that a pedigree is not a substitute for the registration papers. The pedigree is a list of the names of the ancestors and the American Kennel Club will always, for a moderate fee, provide a pedigree if you have the registration papers, *but* they will not register a dog for you even if you do have a pedigree unless you also have the correct papers.

Usually the seller of a puppy provides registration application papers. The Kennel Club issues these when the breeder applies for registration of a litter, one blue certificate for each puppy. The breeder fills out the puppy's sex and color, and the name of the party to whom he sells it. If you are the purchaser, your name will appear on the back. If the breeder has first sold the puppy to someone else, that party must make out a grey transfer, and each subsequent purchaser must do the same until the puppy is registered under his own individual name.

Fill in the name you would like him to have, remembering it's for the rest of his life, at the top of the blue certificate. A second choice is necessary in case the first is unacceptable – another dog may have the same name, for instance. The person who sold it to you will print your name in the proper space and sign it. You must sign your name in the space below provided for that purpose (Section B) and send it to the American Kennel Club with the proper fee. Do this as soon as possible. In the event that you misplace the papers later, you will then be able to apply for duplicates personally. If you have not registered the dog in your name, you will have to go back to the last registered owner, in most cases the registered breeder, and ask him to apply for duplicates. This is often difficult, particularly after the breeder has moved or gone out of business.

If your puppy has already been individually registered with the American Kennel Club, the seller will fill out the transfer on the back and sign it.

Registration in England

In England, the procedure for registering a puppy is not quite the same, but when buying a dog it is equally important to obtain all the registration certificates although they may not be available for a few weeks after the purchase has been effected. First, if both parents are registered at the English Kennel Club and if the registration application form has been signed by the breeder, you as the purchaser should be given the completed form by the vendor, and you must sign this, and send it to the Kennel Club with the necessary fee and your choice of name for the puppy. There will then be no difficulty and the Class I certificate will come to you in about ten days. But be sure you have this form together with a copy of the pedigree when you take possession of your puppy. But if one or both of the parents of the puppy are not registered at the Kennel Club, or if for any reason the breeder has not signed or cannot sign the application, the fee will be exactly double, and you will only be issued a Class II registration certificate.

Quite often you may find that the puppy has already been registered by the breeder or the vendor under their own kennel name. In fact, this is usually the case with wellbred puppies that have a good show potential, the reason being that the breeder or vendor wishes his kennel name to be attached to the puppy if and when it becomes a show winner. In this case, you should be handed the Class I registration certificate and also a transfer form which has been completed on the left hand side by the vendor or breeder in whose name the puppy is registered, and which authorizes the transfer of the puppy from the vendor to you, the purchaser. You should then complete the right hand side of the form and send it to the Kennel Club with the necessary fee.

Where to Buy

There are three sources from which puppies are usually obtained: from the private breeder who probably breeds one or two litters at home from his or her own females; from the large or small kennel where many litters are bred, or from the pet shop where puppies are purchased from outside sources, seldom being bred on the premises.

The private breeder may have one or more extremely wellbred females, and may have paid a sizeable fee for the services of a champion or prize-winning sire. On the other hand, he may have a pedestrian female and have used a mediocre dog belonging to a friend around the corner. But in this case the pedigree will tell the merits of both sire and dam of the puppy you fancy.

It is more than likely, however, that the puppies from this home-bred litter will have received special attention; they will probably have been carefully weaned and reared, and will have been loved and handled right from birth. In our opinion, if the conditions of the home are satisfactory, such a puppy would have certain advantages. He will have been cosseted from birth, he will have seen and got to know humans and have been handled and loved every day of his life, and he will know that human hands are friendly. He will start the first weeks of his life trusting people. As one of a small family of four or five puppies, he will not have had to fight and struggle for his rights in a crowd of twenty or thirty. This should ensure that his temperament is placid and nerve free, for his environment has been working towards it. But if he is nervous despite a protected early puppyhood, it would appear that there is some hereditary instability in his temperament, and such a puppy should be passed over.

In the case of a large kennel, puppyhood can be compared with life at school, for here each puppy must look out for himself. He will spend the greater part of his early life without human companionship, for there is not much time for individual petting in the busy kennel, and humans are seen only at feeding times and during grooming sessions. On the other hand, puppies purchased from a top kennel probably will be bred from excellent stock, both sire and dam being carefully matched from the point of view of genetics, and carefully linebred in order to obtain the best results.

Show kennels as a rule only sell puppies of their own breeding, that is, sired by one of their own stud dogs and bred from one of their bitches. Sometimes they may have puppies for sale which have come to them as picks of litters, that is to say, the kennel owner has allowed the owner of an approved and suitable female to mate her with one of his dogs provided that the best male or female puppy is handed to the owner of the stud dog in lieu of the usual stud fee.

SALLY ANNE THOMPSON

I'll take them all!

So you have the problem of choosing between a homebred and possibly much loved and humanized puppy from the private breeder, and, perhaps, a more selectively bred puppy from a large kennel which might not be so humanized.

From a pet shop you are faced with a different proposition, for here the vendor possibly stocks many breeds of dogs, and may have bought up the surplus specimens from private litters – those, in fact, that may not have been quite good enough for the breeder to sell under his own name as show dogs. However, the dogs for sale are usually cheaper as they are intended to be pet rather than show specimens, and if you are prepared to be extremely careful in your choice, you may very well find a puppy that is a bargain and who will mature into a fine specimen.

From any source, take time to check on how the other dogs are kept, their coat condition and general bloom. Beware of any excessive odor that may be hanging around the place because this can only point to dirty conditions which have been allowed to take hold over a long period.

Medical Examination

Many purchasers ask the vendor if they may have the puppy on approval long enough to take him to a veterinarian to have it officially checked for health and condition. This may be agreed to by the vendor, but equally he may be a little chary of allowing his puppy to be taken from the premises, for after all, a perfectly healthy puppy can pick up an infection in an animal hospital. Such a place is more often for sick dogs than for healthy ones.

Possibly the best middle course is to have the veterinarian visit the puppy on his home ground. It may cost a little more, but it will be worth it. While a veterinarian will be willing to examine your potential purchase – for a fee, of course – he should not be asked for an opinion on any pet shop or kennel as it is considered unethical for a veterinarian to pass this type of judgment. So if your vet is reluctant to make any recommendation, respect his scruples.

Health and Temperament

Now for a few hints on choosing a healthy puppy. There are many things to look for. First of all, do not be in too great a hurry. The natural reaction is to think all the puppies are enchanting, for all Poodle puppies are warm and cuddly, and your only thought will be to get your puppy home and have him to yourself. But simmer down – you have a lot of checking to do first. Usually in a batch of puppies, one or perhaps two puppies will push themselves forward, anxious to nibble your fingers, lick your hands, untie your shoelaces, while another couple may retreat into a corner and sit looking at you rather wistfully. As you move to stroke these little shy ones they may raise a paw which makes them appear even more attractive and in need of your love.

But harden your heart. A retiring puppy has the makings of a nervous dog. When he is past puppyhood his retiring ways may develop into a mean and snappy disposition. So concentrate on the wicked little demon who is all over the place.

Next, examine the puppy for general health, and to do this you should part his coat to check for any visible signs of unwanted livestock such as fleas or lice, or else flecks of scurf which could be caused by external or internal parasites such as worms. Check the back legs, the elbows and the sides of the belly particularly. Also examine the skin of the belly for any small red bites, sores or pustules. See, also, if the skin is elastic. When gently pulled up on the back and then released, it should snap back into position. If it remains flacid and flabby, the puppy is not in very good condition. Similarly, the puppy that has a tight skin and bloated abdomen and is none too well covered on ribs, backbone and haunches, may suffer from worm infestation.

The anus should be inspected. If the rectal opening appears to protrude and is fairly pink and sore-looking, it may indicate either

71

Spend a little time checking the health and temperament of the puppy before you purchase him, and you will be rewarded with a fine companion like this.

The eyes of the puppy are often a good indication of his condition. They should be dark and bright, like those of this champion sired 8½ inch Toy male, Quaker Hill. He is held by his owner, Joan Rosen, of New York.

the presence of worms or a recent stomach upset. Check for an umbilical hernia. If a small hernia is present it will be visible, or it can be felt with the fingers; it will feel and look like a pea in the middle of the skin of the abdomen. Usually such a hernia is not serious, disappearing as a rule when the puppy is a few months old. It may be removed by minor surgery. It is either a small hereditary defect, or, more likely, the result of the dam's using her teeth too zealously to sever the umbilical cord when the puppy was born.

Look well into the puppy's eyes – these should be dark, bright and not watery. Eyes that are dull and deep, giving the puppy a weary and perhaps sad expression, are not healthy. Any small blob of pus in the corner, or any weeping, should be regarded with suspicion.

Next, inspect the ears. Look well into these to see if they are clean and free from excessive hair. Take a sniff at them, for a puppy's ears with incipient canker will have an acrid and unpleasant odor. Fondle the puppy's ears, massaging them gently – and if the puppy leans his head on your hands, screwing his head around, making little grunts, again you may suspect all is not well.

Open his mouth and look at his teeth. They should be sharp, white and even, and his gums should be pink. Any tendency to white gums and a pale whitish tongue is not a healthy sign. The tongue should be rose pink but not brick red.

The nose should be moist and cool; but if the puppy has been racing around, his nose might be hot; in this circumstance, it means nothing. A hot, dry, cracked or crusted nose is an unwelcome condition.

Finally, if possible, the puppy's temperature should be taken. This is done by inserting the blunt end of a greased thermometer for about one inch up the rectal orifice. The normal temperature of a dog is 101.5°, but if the puppy registers 102° this is quite admissible and need cause no worry. Any reading of 102.5° upwards or anything below 100.5° must be suspect. In such a case, it is well to leave the puppy for some time and return later for a re-check.

So far, we have dealt only with the checking needed to prove that the puppy is superficially free from disease and is in normally good condition. It is not possible to tell if he is incubating any infection, as not all illnesses raise temperature as a warning. But you, as a potential dog owner, should be ready to make all these checks, and if you do not do so, no one else is to blame if the puppy turns out to be a not-so-healthy specimen. Any breeder, confident that the puppy he is selling is a nice healthy youngster, will welcome such checking, and any seller who resents or refuses such examination must be regarded with suspicion.

A Poodle should have his own bed in a spot that he can really call his own.

VI Puppy Reception

The great day has come! You and your family are to receive your puppy into your home. There are many matters to be attended to before the new member of the family actually arrives.

Sleeping Quarters

Where shall he sleep? It is quite a big question. Although he is hardy enough to do so. the Poodle is not the kind of dog who should sleep outdoors. for he is essentially a dog who thrives in the house. Possibly the kitchen is a good choice, for it will be warm and cozy. He will need to have his own bed in a spot that he can really call his own. It need not be too elaborate because he is bound to want to chew it up when young.

For the first weeks, a strong cardboard box is suitable; one that measures 12 to 14 inches square would be about right for a Miniature puppy (a larger one for the Standard, and a much smaller one for a Toy). Into this put a piece of soft blanket or rug folded several times until it fits the base of the box. Cut down one side of the box, leaving about two inches as a sill; this will keep the rug tidily inside. When he is snugly curled up in such a box he will really feel it is his own, and he will soon go to it whenever he needs a nap. A cardboard box can so easily be renewed if it gets damaged, or as the puppy grows out of it. Place the box in a corner that is moderately warm and well out of any draft.

If you are able to buy a puppy pen, it will be of the greatest use. But if this is not possible, you may be able to barricade a corner of the room, or perhaps the space under the kitchen table, where you can put the puppy when you want him to go to sleep, or eat his meals – at any rate, somewhere to keep him when you don't want him under your feet. His bed, and some sort of pen for controlling him, will be needed immediately, so have them prepared before you bring the puppy home. Have plenty of newspaper ready for the floor of the pen, and some fresh bedding or blanket aired and ready in case of an accident.

LOUISE VAN DER MEID

Follow the diet to which the puppy has been accustomed, for at least the first week. Then, if you wish to make any changes do so gradually by adding small but increasing amounts of the new food to the old.

Puppy Diet

Next, his diet. If possible, get a diet sheet from the vendor before taking possession of your puppy, so that you are able to have everything he will need ready and waiting for him. It is not wise to change his diet when he comes to you unless there is no alternative. Even if the breeder is not thoughtful enough to have a diet sheet prepared, and nearly all breeders will, get verbal instruction as to what the puppy is used to eating and drinking.

Even if you do not think the diet sheet is very good, follow it for the first week, and then gradually change the feeding plan to incorporate your own ideas. The reason why you should not at once alter the diet is because everything is going to be strange and possibly a little frightening to the new arrival. There is so much to see and hear that is all completely new and confusing. This is sure to have an effect on his nervous system, even though you will be doing everything to minimize the strain and anxiety. Security has been taken away from your puppy for the time being, and he is on his own. There are no brothers and sisters to cuddle up to, or to fight with, and he has no warm mother to reassure him. This will put an excessive strain on his nervous system, and the first thing this anxiety will affect is his digestion. Therefore, it is essential not to complicate matters by altering his diet until he has adjusted himself to his new life.

The feeding of the Poodle under all circumstances is discussed in a later chapter, but to help plan a well-balanced menu, a few hints are given here.

The most important fact to remember is that whatever its diet, the puppy grows best on one which approximates the substance of his mother's milk. Almost all recommended puppy diets completely neglect this important fact. Bitch's milk contains 50% fat on a dry basis, or 9%-13% with the water the milk naturally contains. Always see that your puppy has considerable fat in its diet. This may be in ground meat or even from vegetable oils. But don't overdo it or the effect will be to physic your pup.

He will need five small meals a day between the ages of six to ten weeks, four meals a day from ten weeks to four months, three meals from four to eight months, and two meals from eight to twelve months; thereafter, he will be able to manage well on one meal a day. The puppy, six weeks old, should be fed at approximately four

A dog bed raised several inches from the floor is preferable to just the doubled-up blanket as shown here.

The first few weeks in your home are critical in the development of the puppy's temperament. You must be warm and friendly if he is to identify with you and your family.

hour intervals. Assuming that you will give him his breakfast around eight in the morning, it should be either a small milky drink made with a suitable puppy or baby milk food plus fat, or else a small bowl of cereal and warm rich milk. Since honey is relished, a small spoonful can be added.

Honey is highly recommended for dealing with digestive upsets, and so it cannot be stressed too strongly that the puppy should be introduced to it as early as possible. Most puppies like the sweetness, and apart from the healing properties it contains, often a tablet, pill or capsule, or a medicinal powder can be "wrapped up" in honey for easy swallowing.

77

His next meal will be at midday, and for this the puppy should be given two to four ounces (according to whether it is a Toy, Miniature or Standard) of raw or cooked minced meat with fat included. This should be slightly warm, never frozen or too hot. As alternatives, liver, heart or fish may be given, with a very small quantity of wholemeal bread crumbs or with some finely kibbled puppy biscuit.

His next meal will come along about four o'clock in the afternoon, and consist of a small bowl of warm rich milk, or light cream. He will be ready for another substantial meal around eight in the evening. This should be a repeat of his midday feed, but for a change he would probably relish half to one hard-boiled egg with a small quantity of bread crumbs soaked in a little meat broth; another favorite supper dish is a scrambled egg. Chicken has not been included for the simple reason that most dogs enjoy this dish above all others, and having tasted chicken, will refuse all other food. So be warned, and guard against its becoming the ruling factor of your dog's diet.

His final meal will be at bedtime and should consist of a large bone to gnaw (one with no sharp corners or edges, or splinters that can be torn off), and this should keep him busy until he cuddles down to sleep. When he is very young he may also be given a small milky drink on going to bed, but in the interests of night cleanliness this may be discontinued when he is nine weeks old. As an alternative to the bone, a wholemeal biscuit may be given, or else two fingers of toast, lightly buttered. There must, of course, be a bowl of clean, fresh water always in the same place so that he knows exactly where to go to get his drink. Chicken, rabbit, fish or chop bones are all highly dangerous to the dog and the puppy. Only large beef bones may be given safely.

As the puppy grows older, he will lose interest in his breakfast, so this should be the first feed discontinued. Soon after, a mid-afternoon drink will not be necessary, and finally, he will do extremely well on one large meal a day, or two smaller meals. This is true for the large Standard as well as the small Toy.

Bringing the Puppy Home

Possibly you and all your family will want to go to collect the puppy. After you have exhaustively checked all that is necessary regarding the health conditions and structure of the puppy, the journey home will start, probably in your own automobile. The puppy may be sick because this may be the first time he has been in a car and experienced its motion, and also, he is bound to be a little over excited. So it may be best to take a small traveling box, or cardboard box with you for the journey home. At any rate, arm yourself with a damp sponge and some paper towels.

You must keep in mind that everything is now very strange to him. He has suddenly become someone exceptional, to be fondled and played with, and talked to unendingly. Perhaps he has previously lived in a kennel; now there is furniture to be dealt with, and a world full of human feet! It is all so different – there are no other puppies about, and the smells are all so strange. In fact, for a few days and nights, life is going to be very difficult. And in order to cope with this sudden busy life, the puppy must have plenty of undisturbed rest. Make it a rule to shut him in his pen for a full hour after each of his three solid meals, and to see that he is never awakened suddenly. In fact, it is far better if he is allowed to wake up quietly in his own good time, but this is not always possible. So if it is essential to awaken him, stroke him gently until he stirs. But never, *never* pick him up suddenly when he is fast asleep. This can have a bad effect on both his nerves and his heart, and could easily turn him into a nervous, apprehensive dog. Also, don't overplay with him for long periods. Puppies are like children, for if they are overexcited and overstimulated, they become irritable, nervous, and too tired to sleep normally at night. So, for you own peace, never let him get overexcited.

Night Training

The first night is very important for both you and the puppy. The enthusiasm of the family for the new pet will wane quickly if no one can get any rest because the puppy raises his voice querulously during the night.

Give him a box that he cannot climb out of. Make a nest in the middle and put in it a bed warmer of some sort, either a warmed brick or a hot water bottle. When you put the puppy to bed, remove the bed warmer and pop him into the warm nest. Cover the top of the box with a rug, leaving plenty of room for ventilation, and leave him decisively, preferably in the dark. Alternatively, place a large, upturned box over his bed, but be very sure that a gentle current of air is flowing. If you have made these preparations, you should have success. His belly is pleasantly full, he is warm, he cannot get out of his bed and become cold and lost in the dark, and he will soon fall asleep, giving the household a peaceful night. He may exercise his vocal powers for five minutes or so, but he will soon settle down. The authors have rarely known this treatment to fail.

It is best not to start any real training until the puppy has had a chance to "re-locate". His little brain will be spinning with his new routine, and one cannot expect him to take in much more for the time being. We shall be talking about his ultimate training in the next chapter.

There are two points to be dealt with concerning the new puppy. These are the treatment for eradicating worms, and immunizing "shots" to protect him from disease and infection.

Worming

All puppies should have their initial worm dose at seven or eight weeks of age or earlier. Sometimes it may be necessary, in the case of a heavy infestation, to worm at five to six weeks of age, but this is not advisable if it can be avoided. Very, very occasionally a puppy may be really riddled with worms, losing weight and condition and even suffering convulsions at the age of three weeks. It may prove extremely dangerous, even fatal. Nonetheless, the puppy may die as a result of the worms, and it is therefore simply a matter of kill or cure. But this extreme condition happens only rarely, and usually only in puppies bred under shocking conditions from parents who are themselves completely worm infested.

TOM CARAVAGLIA

Mike-Mar's Dandy Boy is a 2 year old cafe-au-lait Miniature, shown here in sporting clip. Sired by American Champion Field-stream Valentine, he is a fine example of an excellent companion dog whose owner, Mrs. Lillian Grossman of New York, has never bothered to show him.

Ouch, those shots hurt!　　　　　A life-long attachment.

It is a wise precaution to give the dam a worm dose ten days after she has been mated. Most puppies that are born with worms received them prenatally from their mother. The signs that a puppy may be harboring worms are many and various. They can affect the appetite, which may either be voracious or "choosey", or alternate between the two from day to day. The stomach may be large or blown out ("pot bellied") and the rest of the body thin and bony. His stools may be loose, and rather mucousy. His coat may be flat and staring, the reverse of crisp and shining. He may drag along the floor on his bottom, although this alone does not mean the presence of worms – it might simply point to a slight irritation or chapped condition of the anus. The eyes may be a little cloudy and deep looking and the breath offensive. Obviously, the symptoms that will tell you most are the worms themselves in the stools or vomit. Roundworms will be coiled tight, slightly pinkish in color, usually five to six inches long, and the width of a piece of fine string, tapered at each end. They resemble limp spaghetti.

Most puppies will have been treated for worms by the breeder before you take delivery, but some breeders may omit this necessary dosing. One must always remember that a dog can become re-infested after being wormed. In any case, the puppy will need a second worm dose at twelve to fourteen weeks, but it is strongly recommended that advice be sought from a veterinarian who can prescribe the correct dose for the age and weight and general physical condition of the puppy. Worms are an ailment that must be accepted in puppies, and a cure is usually quickly effected.

Inoculations

The next important step in the puppy's life is immunization against disease. Infection is always just around the corner until the young puppy has been inoculated. They are naturally protected from disease for the first six weeks of their lives because they receive immunity through the mother's milk, provided of course that she herself has been fully inoculated. The first fluid produced in her milk after whelping, is called colostrum. This is normal bitch's milk but it also contains globulin which provides the puppies with antibodies and confers temporary immunity.

Puppies that are hand reared, and so deprived of their mother's milk, must be given other forms of immunization in the form of gammaglobulin; the veterinarian will advise. After six to seven weeks this immunization will wear off, but as a certain amount will remain in the puppy's blood stream until he is eleven or twelve weeks of age, he must wait for his regular inoculation until then. So between seven and twelve weeks of age he is particularly open to infection, and should under no circumstances be allowed out in public. He should be kept strictly within his own dwelling place or grounds where there is no danger that other dogs have left any infection.

Recent research indicates that the use of a live vaccine even as early as six weeks of age will afford some protection. This should be followed by another "shot" when he is between eleven and twelve weeks old.

At about twelve weeks, he should have immunizing shots to protect him against such diseases as Hard Pad, Distemper, Infectious Hepatitis and Leptospirosis. This may entail just one injection, or, at most, a second one fourteen days later. Such inoculation usually gives complete immunization for from one year to eighteen months, and sometimes for life. Some veterinarians advise that a yearly booster should be given.

Puppies do need vitamin supplements when the diet is incomplete during the growing period, particularly so during the winter months. There are many such supplements on the market which are excellent.

But really good feeding, clean conditions, and sound common sense is all that is needed to rear your small puppy to happy adulthood. Don't leave anything to chance. Particularly when he is young, plan in advance for his healthy, happy life.

Poodles and cats are not natural enemies, as proved by this picture. It is preferable that they be introduced at an early age. However, with a little care and forethought, even older animals will learn to tolerate each other.

VII Training the Poodle Puppy

We are now assuming that your Poodle has settled down in your home and established himself as one of the family. It is now the moment to think seriously about his training, because if he is to remain a favorite with the household, he has much to learn. But the Poodle has an alert brain; he can think things out for himself, and, provided his training is carefully planned and carried out, he will readily cooperate.

The great danger in training is that if it is continued for too long at a time the Poodle will lose interest. Once you have lost his interest, it is no use going on. You must give up and start again next day. But an efficient and inspired trainer will not put himself in this position; he will not lose his dog's interest. The golden rule is plenty of praise and encouragement, and short training periods.

Social Behavior

Recent genetic studies emphasize the importance of heredity in the development of dog behavior. Heredity has an important effect on almost every trait tested. This study was by Drs. J. P. Scott and John L. Fuller, working at the Jackson Laboratory, Bar Harbor, Maine. They worked with five breeds of dogs representing the major groups: Wire-Hair Fox Terrier, American Cocker Spaniel, African Basenji, Shetland Sheepdog and the Beagle.

Among other things, they found that sex does have definite effects upon the aggressive tendencies of dogs and upon the dominance order, but not upon their trainability and ability to solve problems. This means then that the male is more dominant (the pack leader) and aggressive, but that the female is his equal when it comes to training and intelligence,

Inherited emotional traits profoundly influence performance. Although the various breeds differed widely in emotional and motivational characteristics, no one breed was superior to any other in

"Oh, he floats through the air with the greatest of ease." These words might indeed have been written about our friend the Poodle. This trick is not recommended for any other than a well-trained animal, but it does illustrate the agility that has made the Poodle so famous as a trick and circus performing dog.

SALLY ANNE THOMPSON

solving problems. Detailed statistical analyses indicate that there is a highly complete relationship between the basic genetic inheritance and its final effect upon behavior.

Perhaps the most important of their findings so far as the pet owner is concerned is that there is a critical period in the puppy's life which exerts a lasting influence upon its adult behavior and ability to adjust to human relationships. A puppy removed from its mother and littermates at the age of six to eight weeks, and brought into a home and family environment, where it is handled and petted, has a far better chance of becoming a well-adjusted dog in its relationships with both people and other dogs than the one left behind in the kennel where, although it is adequately fed and housed, it is not given the advantage of human handling. For a puppy to turn out well then, it should be brought into the home as early as possible (before it is eight weeks old) and certainly not after 13 weeks if it has never known the human touch. Let me emphasize that this contact with humans need not necessarily be extensive. Even picking a dog up gently once a day is sufficient to establish the proper rapport.

Understanding His Name

Perhaps you've bought a pedigreed Poodle with a name as long as a French Count's. That's for his registration papers. Give him a call name for everyday use. Make it short – preferably one syllable; if longer, with at least one heavily accented syllable – and one that sounds like no other in the household. Insist that everyone stick to this agreed-on name. Use it whenever you call him. Avoid "Come here, boy!" unless Boy is the name you have chosen. When you reward him, do it while using his name. But when you scold him do not use it because he should never consider his name as a warning of punishment.

Most pups learn their names along with housebreaking. Nevertheless, a bit of special name-training in the early days will make later training easier.

Housebreaking

The very first training to be tackled, obviously, is housebreaking. No one in the household is going to take kindly to frequent puddles and messes all over the house, and the quicker the puppy learns control, the better everyone will like it.

So, as soon as your puppy has had a short period to settle himself into his new routine, the business of housebreaking must commence. Since Poodles have a wealth of intelligence, this problem can be completely overcome within a week – indeed, many Poodle puppy owners say they have never had any housebreaking difficulty. But this depends on how you, yourself, apply the training. You must be systematic, always regular and very patient. It is a tiring job but it pays in the end. Praise and shame are the keynotes of the training. The Poodle is extremely fond of praise, and will do anything to please his owner. He has as well a pronounced sense of shame, and will mind far more your voice of displeasure than he will a sharp rap on the haunch. So be lavish in your praise when he has done his duty in the appointed place, and stinging in your displeasure when an accident occurs – particularly stinging when the accident is obviously intentional!

For those who have a yard, this training will not be too difficult. In England, housebreaking does not present quite such a problem, as nearly every house or bungalow has a small yard (or garden, as it is called) attached.

Outdoor Training

But to return to the actual training, we will talk first to those owners who have a yard where the puppy may be put to learn his manners. It is really no use slapping a puppy for making a mess because he just doesn't understand. As yet, he has neither the intelligence nor the muscular control to wait while *you* finish what you are doing before you take him out. Consequently, if he makes a puddle on your best rug, it may be your fault, not his!

Try to take him out to the same patch of grass or earth immediately after he wakes up from a nap, and before and after each meal. At first you may have to wait around for quite a while, and he will probably strain your patience to the utmost by either gaily playing, or by just sitting looking up at you, wondering what you want! As soon as he has performed, however, reward him with a small tidbit and be lavish with your praise. It does not do the slightest bit of good to put him out *after* he has made a mistake, but if you actually catch him in the act, a good scolding and a quick pushing out of the door into the yard, may, by association of ideas, give him the message. But restraint is difficult for the puppy before he has learned some measure of control because he doesn't know in advance that it is going to happen, and so he suddenly squats down wherever he happens to be, with little warning. Equally, when he uses the place that you want him to use, he will soon associate both the smell and the location with the idea that this is the proper place, and that he will be praised and petted whenever he uses it.

Paper Training

It is not always possible to take a puppy out at just the strategic second, and so a puppy play pen has much to recommend it. The pen should surround his bed, and the floor covered with newspaper. He must learn to do his business on the newspaper in the pen. He can then sleep in this pen, and when he gets up in the night, as he undoubtedly will, he will realize that if the newspaper is used it will be permitted, but going anywhere else in the house is forbidden, the penalty being a scolding.

But if you live in an apartment with no yard, paper training is essential, because no puppy should be allowed on the street until he is completely immunized, and such immunization, as we have already said, is not usually carried out until the puppy is three months old.

Adult dogs are naturally clean and fastidious animals; in fact, they will often go out of your sight before performing their natural functions. Puppies, on the other hand, do have frequent calls of nature, and never know when they are going to come. What is objectionable to you is perfectly natural to them. But as soon as a puppy begins to learn that it displeases you, he will try to learn control.

Evacuation must be expected as often as four times a day; in fact, after each meal, and urination even more often. The paper to be used for training always means newspaper, and not shredded news-sheet nor crumpled newspaper, but sheets of newsprint spread on the floor several pages thick. The more absorbent the paper, the better, and you must avoid using magazine pages or Sunday supplements, for they do not absorb well. Paper towels are excellent but very expensive for this purpose; they do have the advantage of easy disposal.

At first, the paper may be spread wherever the puppy normally has his freedom, but this freedom should be carefully limited. again by the use of a play pen. He may be allowed access to other parts of the house for short periods of play, but only *after* you are sure he has performed his functions. Frequently a puppy forms an attachment for a particular spot for his misdemeanors – quite often behind a sofa, or on a particular doormat, or a bedside rug where he thinks it doesn't show! Once you have located this secret hide-out, place many sheets of paper there. When the association of newspaper and the call of nature has been formed, the newspaper can be gradually moved each day a little nearer to an area that is more convenient for you.

Soiled papers should be removed immediately, though it may be a bright idea to leave on slightly stained sheet to act as a reminder. Many pet shops have housebreaking sprays on sale; these are very helpful, and when sprayed on a sheet of newspaper, attract the puppy to use it immediately.

Poodles seldom require extreme punishment. Usually, a sad and disappointed tone of voice has a more lasting effect. American Champion Jacques, a show and house dog, is too well-behaved to require reprimanding.

TOM CARAVAGLIA

A puppy usually has to relieve himself as soon as he wakes. There is usually a large yawn and then a squatting down. If the puppy is kept in a confined space overnight (and this really is an excellent idea), place him immediately in a play pen on newspapers, and keep him there until he has done his "jobs".

It is also important to work out, and keep to, a regular feeding schedule so that you may anticipate his urges. Shortly after he has eaten, usually within ten minutes, his bowels will work and he should be kept in the pen and on newspaper until they have. Then it will be safe (or nearly safe!) to give him his freedom throughout the house for a scamper and a good game. He will soon learn this routine, too, and want to play his part.

When a mistake is made, carry the puppy to the spot and point it out to him. Shame him as if he were a naughty child. A smart slap on the rump with a rolled up newspaper will help to make your point, but with a Poodle a sad and disappointed tone of voice seems to have a more lasting effect. Any soiled places must be scrubbed without delay with a strong detergent of disinfectant, so that any lingering odor will not attract him again to the spot. Ammonia or vinegar are both excellent deodorizers.

Street Training

When the Poodle has had his "shots", and is fully immunized against disease, he may begin his outdoor and curb training. Some people recommend that all newspaper be dispensed with at this point, while others suggest that the newspapers gradually be concentrated at a spot close to the outside door, and then under the door with just one corner showing, finally disappearing altogether.

Happy is the dog owner who can just open the kitchen door and let his puppy run out into the yard. But most dog owners have to dress in haste, put the lead on the Poodle and hurry him out of the house almost before they are fully awake, and certainly before drinking that first cup of coffee. During the initial nine months of the puppy's life, this routine must be endured at least five times a day. The Poodle must be taken out immediately on waking, after each feed (and these will number three), and then finally before he goes to bed – and that makes five! As the Poodle grows up, these outings can be reduced to three, for he will only need the one meal a day.

When you have passed the stage of newspaper, more than ever a young Poodle will need to be either in his pen, or tied by his lead to a radiator or a screw eye in a baseboard, or at any rate kept under constant supervision, until he is absolutely to be relied on, with no danger of a lapse. It is the easiest thing in the world for a young dog to fall back into bad habits, and these are twice as difficult to break. But a leashed dog will very seldom soil his immediate surroundings, and practically never soil his own bed. Certainly it helps if the Poodle is kept in a large box from which he cannot get out during the night, and most Poodles like this form of night sleep. A well ventilated wooden box dropped like a cake cover over his pad or blanket works well, for it keeps him warm and free of drafts, and in the dark. But he must be freed early in the morning as soon as he begins to stir, and taken out immediately. A puppy must never be tied by a leash unsupervised. It is far too easy for him to strangle himself. Every leash should have a swivel.

While a puppy is learning his outdoor manners and curb training, he must be made to understand that these outings are strictly for business, not pleasure. Allow him to remain outdoors for about ten minutes. or until he has relieved himself, and then take him back. If he has done his duty, praise and make much of him. But if he has been stubborn and wasted your time, show your displeasure, and put him either in the play pen or else tie him up by his leash until you can take him out again. When you are breaking him, always try to take him to the same spot, for dogs develop a liking for a special place, and this is generally a place used by other dogs.

If you cannot, or do not wish to let your Poodle off his regular lead, use a long piece of cord or rope, so that he may have the maximum freedom possible, for he will like to sniff about and choose his spot. Smells mean much to the Poodle, and he should not be pulled away from a good "sniffy" tree or post, unless it is obviously polluted in some way. When he has staked his claim on a special place, take him to that same place every day, encouraging him when you get here. He will soon learn what is required of him, and function immediately.

It helps a great deal to be regular in the times you take your Poodle out: he will adjust himself to these set times, and learn to contain himself until then. But because he can only restrain himself for a reasonable period, it is essential not to make him wait too long. It may be very painful for him to wait, and it certainly is not fair. The older dog. although well-trained, may occasionally be "taken

Poodles were originally bred to assist duckhunters, and even today many of them are natural retrievers. All they need is a little encouragement.

short", but since he is normally so good-mannered, this is obviously a situation beyond his control. The signs will be a distressed and almost panic-stricken expression on his face while he turns around quickly in tight circles. There may still be time to pick him up and get him outside, or else again, the handy newspaper will come into use. But in such circumstances, don't chastise him; ignore him instead. By now he is far too well-trained to do such a dreadful thing for choice – in fact, he had no *other* choice!

In the big cities, it is essential that a dog learn to defecate in the gutter or by the curb. In most places, a dog owner can be fined for allowing his dog to foul the sidewalk. It is an unpleasant situation when dogs foul the bus stops, or the paths of parks, and urinate against shop fronts, doors of houses, and against automobile tires. This is carelessness on the part of the owner that shows a lack of consideration for others. A dog quickly learns that the gutter is the right place, especially if he is kept on a leash until he has done his duty, and is carefully guided there by his owner.

It has been observed that male puppies urinate more frequently than female puppies, and that both sexes particularly lack control while cutting their second teeth. But once the teething period is over, matters improve.

Young puppies at the age of nine to fourteen weeks often have an irritating and embarrassing habit of not being able to hold their water when picked up and made a fuss of. It is very trying when a stream occurs on picking up your puppy to fondle him. The same thing can happen when he is wriggling around your feet with pleasure; you suddenly find your shoe full of warm wetness. It is a phase of adolescence that disappears with time.

Very occasionally, an adult dog when left alone may wet in his owner's slipper, or on some piece of clothing bearing the owner's smell. This is done as a protest against being left alone, or to establish the fact that the person concerned belongs to him. Some dogs, when they have completed their meal, will turn around and make a puddle in the empty dish. This is a throw back to olden days when a wild dog would establish ownership of his property by leaving his mark in this way. But it is far from a pleasant habit, and it must be discouraged.

The Poodle, should he develop such tricks, can be shamed out of them quite quickly.

Urinary Behavior

Young puppies of both sexes squat to urinate. With the female this attitude persists through life, but with the male it changes at puberty. As they mature sexually, males begin to lift a hind leg and direct their urine against some object – the long-suffering tree and fire hydrant, for instance. At this time too, they begin to urinate more frequently, and to "hold back," expelling only a little urine at a time and distributing it over a wide area, thus leaving a trail wherever they go. This serves to mark the boundary of the individual dog's territory. In the wild stage, it served to inform any stray animal that "this land is mine."

Males can differentiate between the odor of masculine and feminine urine; they can also detect whether or not the female is in heat. Sometimes an old bitch or one that has been spayed will urinate like a male.

Furniture "Breaking"

It is not uncommon for a dog to plant himself on choice comfort spots like armchairs, beds and sofas. Some dogs even hog the hearth, denying its warmth to the family members. Get on to your Poodle right from the start. When he jumps up on a chair or bed, push him off. Use the word "No" with considerable emphasis and guide him to a spot that you have decided is his. Perhaps a mat or small rug can be kept there for him to relax on. If you are consistent in this right from the beginning he will quickly catch on to what is "verboten". If not, and a firmer approach is needed, make a news-paper baton. This is simply a rolled up newspaper taped at the ends and used as a "whip" – not to swat the dog with, but to crack down beside him. If the baton is not close at hand at the critical moment, toss a book or magazine just close enough to miss him. This will startle him off the forbidden spot. Most dogs view the human ability to throw with great respect. They find it something they cannot easily retaliate, and this kind of action usually wins the day. Commercially-prepared repellent sprays are also available.

Some trainers recommend other devices. One is a tack-board: a piece of cardboard impregnated with a few thumb tacks. It is placed on the chair or sofa and a piece of fabric thrown over it. The dog jumps up – ouch! He doesn't jump again. Another gimmick is a tin tray of empty cans balanced on the arm of the sofa. It falls with a loud clatter when the dog jumps up. Still another trick is the use of mouse-traps (not rat-traps). These snap and startle the dog but are not powerful enough to hurt him. A "toss-bomb" can also be made. This is a small juice can in which are sealed a few bolts and nuts. One is kept in every room where the dog might offend. It is tossed to land at his feet when he is least expecting it!

Collar and Leash

Sometimes the Poodle owner may experience considerable difficulty in teaching his Poodle to walk on a lead. There is no doubt that Poodles are lovable, companionable, and have a delightful sense of humor – but they can be obstinate! We must face this fact. The endeavor of trying to get a Poodle puppy to walk on a collar and lead may well try the patience of the most saintly owner.

Buy your puppy a narrow, rolled leather collar to begin with, one that can be let out as he grows. See that this collar is not on too tight by checking it at least once a week. A wide collar decorated with colored stones may be suitable when the puppy is older, but for the young one it may be cumbersome. The show puppy should wear

At exciting moments like this, a Poodle can hardly be blamed for barking in sheer delight. He just loves attention and wants to tell the world about it. A certain amount of this is understandable. However, the habit of constant or senseless barking should be discouraged at an early age,

a collar only when he is going out. At all other times, and especially at night, one should not be worn because it will rub the hair and do damage to the show coat. A very thin rolled collar is the only type suitable for the show dog. A light chain is often chosen for the pet Poodle, and it looks very nice, but here again, it will rub down a runway around the neck.

To introduce the puppy to his collar, fasten it around his neck and leave it on for just a few minutes. He is bound to scratch at it to begin with. Put the collar on for a slightly longer period every day until he takes it for granted. This is fairly easy; it is the leash that presents a difficulty. Training some Poodles to the leash will take a lot of time and patience, while others will offer no objections at all, and walk normally on the first try-out.

The best way is clip the leash on to the collar and then let it drop. Let the puppy trail it around for ten minutes at a time for a couple of days. When you think he is fairly well used to it, pick it up and call him. If he does not come, give a slight tug. He may follow you. But he may also sit down stubbornly, or make an exhibition of himself by rolling on his back, kicking and biting the leash. In which case, drop it and walk away, completely ignoring him. Poodles hate being ignored; it really upsets their dignity, so after several minutes you will probably find him sidling up to you trailing the hated leash. Pick it up again, and if he comes with you, even reluctantly, make a great fuss over him and then take the leash off, letting him run free.

The next day, the exercise must be repeated but always remember to drop the lead, turn your back and walk away if he is uncooperative. He will learn in time, especially if he knows that good behavior means a good walk with plenty of free running along with the leashing.

Never leave a Poodle tied to a post or any object for more than a few seconds if you are not there. He can so easily wind himself around a table leg or a post until he strangles himself. Never leave a Poodle tied up on a high table or a chair, and never leave him tied to the wheel of your automobile – it is too easy for him to fall or jump off and hang himself. A Poodle, however, must come to realize that there will be times when he is tied up, for the show Poodle must be leashed to his bench during a show, and will almost certainly be leashed at the Grooming Parlor while awaiting his turn for clipping.

There are many other lessons that your Poodle must learn if he is to be a pleasant companion in the home, and appreciated by all who live there. So often, though, a puppy is indulged tremendously when young, and then suddenly scolded for doing the very same things that up 'til then were referred to as "cute". For the sake of the puppy, teach him to behave well from the start; it is far easier on him. The chances are he may develop several sins. such as barking for no reason at all, chewing up everything he comes across, and jumping up at people from sheer joy.

Senseless Barking

Constant barking is a dreadful habit; one that causes endless trouble and irritation to both yourself and your neighbors, and such a habit must be broken as soon as it manifests itself. Such barking may easily start as a protest at being left alone, or it may ensue from boredom. First, the puppy should have a toy box containing a variety of interesting objects like a hard rubber ball, a chew stick, a felt or rubber toy, a small cardboard box, a ball of crushed paper (not newspaper), a strip or rag knotted tightly and as many other fascinating things as you can think of. This toy box should be given to him as is, not unpacked, whenever you want to leave him alone. He will spend a lot of time unpacking it and playing with the toys, and then he will probably tire and go quickly to sleep. But these toys should only be given when you have to leave him, and must come as a treat. Otherwise, they will lose their novelty.

But, of course, you will not want to restrain your Poodle from legitimate barking for there are many times when a little noise is more than justified. For instance, the very presence of a barking dog in the house will often deter the intending burglar, so somehow you must instill into the Poodle that some people are "friends" and some are "foes."

A dog should always be allowed to bark when the doorbell rings, and certainly at night he should be encouraged to do so; but on a command from his owner he should realize that here is no danger and to stop barking. To emphasize your point, take hold of his muzzle and give the special command to be quiet; he will then be unable to bark. Of course, he will bark again as soon as your hand is removed, but persevere, and he will relate the word you use to your hand holding his muzzle, and before long stop when told to. This must be taught from an early age; the words employed are a matter of choice. They can be "No", "Stop", "Friend", or anything else, but it is an advantage to use a pair of words for "no barking" so that the Poodle gets a picture in his mind conjured up by this situation alone. If it is a routine word like "No", or "Quiet," used for other situations, it is apt to cause confusion in the dog's mind.

So match words to specific situations; therein lies success. You will find that your Poodle is really very clever, able to add more and more words to his ever growing vocabulary, and before long the only thing that will surprise you is his never speaking back!

"And a little child shall lead them. . ."

Chewing

A destructive puppy can be another menace in the home. While this applies only to the puppy less than a year old, a lot of damage can be done in twelve months. Chewing is enjoyed because new teeth are coming through, and they are helped along by continual gnawing. If you provide the puppy with something else to gnaw and chew he is less likely to destroy your shoes, your slippers, the upholstered arm of your sofa, the leg of a prized antique chair. Again give him plenty of large beef bones, chew sticks and various other things which have no resemblance to the valuable articles he might fancy. But on the whole, Poodles are not destructive if they are given things which they know are their's to chew.

Jumping Up

Another irritating habit is the Poodles bouncing up to everyone with an excess of spirit. Not everyone appreciates such a welcome, particularly so if it is a rainy day and the Poodle's paws are caked with mud. Again, another special word to suit the occasion is needed. The word "Down" is frequently used. But this may not be enough for the over excitable puppy, so a smart slap with a rolled up newspaper will be needed to cast him down both physically and mentally. A knee raised as he is about to jump has a good effect, as it bumps his nose.

Gnawing

If he is the kind of puppy who will not leave off gnawing your hands and fingers, the best way to restrain him is to pinch in his cheeks with your other hand. He will then find himself nipping the inside of his own mouth and stop immediately. If this trick is repeated every time the gnawing begins, he will soon get over the habit.

But it must be stressed yet again that the Poodle is intelligent and able to build up to thoroughly understanding a large vocabulary of commands. He longs to please, and can be quelled more by words and tone of voice than by any vigorous action. A rolled up newspaper will discipline him more than any other form of chastisement, and do no physical or mental harm, whereas some of the more drastic methods employed to teach other breeds could well damage the Poodle – if not physically, then beyond doubt temperamentally.

Biting

Growling and biting are serious and objectionable faults in dogs. They can be cured with simple little lessons which can be given to puppies from the time they are weaned. Growling at the food dish is probably the first bad habit that a puppy gets. And he usually starts by growling at his littermates. He must be taught, however, not to resent his owners.

Most people find this growling at the food dish has not been cured by the breeder, and so they have to take over. Do this by reaching down to interfere with the puppy's feeding. When he growls, you say "No!," grab him by the tail and jerk him away from the food dish, almost rolling him across the floor. He will be startled and surprised by this sudden action.

While you have his attention, caution him, and then let him return to his food. Or, you may give the stern "No" while flicking his nose with your middle finger and thumb.

In either case, the puppy should learn that he must not growl at or try to bite members of the family, and that it remains for you to say when he can eat. The lesson is not hard to teach, but it requires repetition a time or two at each meal until trials show you that the puppy accepts this as one of the "house rules."

All puppies like to rough house. But puppies soon bite too hard, and their teeth are very sharp. They also tend to get angry. Your procedure is to play with your puppy until he does get angry and bites too hard. Then you must scold him; and perhaps even punish him, saying "No bite!" several times.

He must learn not to go too far in play, and that he can never growl or bite a human being. You'll be amazed at how quickly he'll learn this if you arrange lessons so that he gets one or two a day.

Don't Steal!

Some dogs are honest and some are not. Teach yours that the first rule of dog etiquette is not to steal from the table. You can do this by scolding him whenever he shows any interest in food on the table. If he persists then deliberately place food near the table edge with set mouse traps in front of it. Make your "plant" in such a way that the dog will spring the traps before he can reach the food. One or two lessons like this will usually do the trick and you won't have to worry about a breach of good manners again.

Outdoor Manners

Inside the house, your dog's behavior can be whatever you are willing to put up with. But once he's outside, you have a responsibility to the community. Don't let your dog become the neighborhood pest.

Speak to Go Out!

Some dogs seem to do this almost automatically; others have to be taught. Put your dog inside the door while you step outside. He'll want to join you. Open the door a crack. Command "Speak" in an excited voice, even making a barking noise; anything to get the dog excited. Repeat again and again and all of a sudden, your dog will let out a bark. Instantly open the front door and praise him lavishly. Practice doing this from inside as well as out, so that the dog learns to bark for passage either way.

Yard Breaking

Teach your dog to use only a certain portion of your own yard – behind or beside the garage, or out behind the shrubbery. You can

By holding a tidbit just above his head, he will learn to stand on his hind legs on command. By revolving your hand slowly, he will also learn to dance. This should only be done with an older dog whose back muscles have matured.

do this by placing some of his droppings there, then taking him to that spot when you know it is necessary. When he relieves himself there, praise him.

Meanwhile, spray any other yard spot he has used previously with a good commercial deodorant. The smell will keep your dog away from those areas, and he will start using the area you have chosen for him.

If you fence the area you have selected, you can leave your dog there for an hour or so at regular times each day.

To keep this area clean, droppings should be disposed of regularly. They can be placed in the street sewer or used in your garden as manure. Various scoop-type gadgets are sold which make it easy to pick up and dispose of the droppings.

Running Away

If, during training for the previous lesson, the dog decides to run away, it will be necessary for you to catch and punish him, then to send him home. However, never call the dog to you and then punish him. This will make him hesitate to come to you the next time you call. Punish him only when you have to go after and catch him. After you have hauled the dog back into your yard, you can praise him, so that he'll know he's a good dog when he's in his own yard.

Digging Holes

Dogs often dig holes because of sheer boredom. Occassionally they'll dig just for exercise, but it all stems from an age-old habit of digging for moles, chipmunks, or other game. You can keep your dog from digging again in a hole by placing two or three set mousetraps in the hole. The hole can also be filled with crumpled up chicken wire, well pegged down. Dogs don't like to dig against wire. You can also fill the hole with large stones which he can't move.

The dog will probably dig another hole. But if your repeat the above corrective procedures he'll soon get discouraged.

Sometimes dogs dig holes in very hot weather in order to lie in the cool ground. When this is the cause, bring the dog into the house.

Meet the Mailman

Properly brought up pups just don't get the idea that it's permissible to bite the mailman or meter reader. Highly nervous dogs, dogs that are kept tied up for long periods, and basically shy dogs who attack out of fear attempt to bite these men or other strangers.

You should introduce your dog to mailmen and meter readers. These men should be encouraged to give the dog bits of food and a chance to smell and investigate them thoroughly. Ask them to call the dog by name and greet him with praise, plus tidbits each time they come, until they are accepted as friends.

The food bribes can be eliminated except for an occasional treat once a friendship has been established. It is also a good idea to learn when these calls are made and if possible bring the dog into the house ahead of time. You can thus reassure your dog that all is well.

During the summer many dog shows are held out-of-doors, creating a gay and festive occasion. This show is taking place in England, but the scene would be the same anywhere in the world where dogs come together in show competition.

VIII   The Poodle in the Show Ring

Early Training

For show ring training, the Poodle is never too young to start. The first lesson begins at the age of eight weeks when he should be given at least one of his meals while standing on a steady table. He should be taught to stand quietly with his four legs at the correct show angle, and then the dish of food should be held at such a height that he must stretch his neck upwards to get the pieces out of it. At the same time, his tail should be stroked upwards so that it stands in an erect position. This lesson should be repeated every day for several weeks. When four months old, he can be fed on the floor, but with his dish on a stand raised several inches, so that again he must stretch his neck and hold his head high. This also prevents him from turning his elbows out, as, of necessity, he must stand well up on his toes to reach his dinner.

Another early exercise is to stand the puppy on a table with hind-quarters well stretched back, tail up, front legs straight and parallel, and head erect. This show stance can be achieved by holding the puppy in the correct position with both hands, and then taking them away while telling the puppy to "Stay" or "Stand." If this exercise is repeated every day he will quickly learn to adopt this correct show stance every time he stands.

Leash Training

The show puppy must also be given collar and leash training early in life. An area should be appointed either in your yard or indoors which can be regarded as a show ring for training purposes. In this special area the Poodle puppy must be taught to walk steadily on leash at his trainer's left side. He should be walked up the imaginary ring for about twelve yards, walking out to his full capacity, tail up, head up, and at the top he should stop, turn about and then walk back again. He should then be walked across the ring and back again; having walked across on your left side, he must learn to walk back on your right side, so that he is always on the side nearest to the judge. Some Poodles who have not been taught to walk on both sides will only walk on the left, and this often puts the handler between the Poodle and the judge, completely obscuring the dog.

Handling

The next exercise, but one to be commenced only after the puppy has had his shots and is fully immunized, is to get him used to being handled by all and sundry. It is of no use if the show puppy can only be handled by those he knows, or those of one particular sex. The judge will want to examine him from nose to tail, looking at his teeth, examining his tail carriage, feeling him for width of chest and spring of ribs, picking up a leg and examining his feet and toes. When the judge stares into your Poodle's eyes, there must be no shrinking or pulling back. He must learn to gaze straight back at the judge. Your Poodle must learn to accept all this as a matter of course, and the only way to teach him is to run through all exercises daily until they become routine. But especially, you must get all your friends of both sexes to handle him, and the doctor, the milkman, the garage man as well. Ask them all to feel his coat, to press on his back to test his resistance, to touch his ears and his tail, and to look him straight in the eyes. As a result he will take it in stride when the judge does the same things at a show.

He must learn to walk up and down among other dogs, and to turn a deaf ear to the various little snaps and growls and flurries of temper that may occur. He must pass other dogs by as though they did not exist. So, in order to get him used to these slightly upsetting moments, he should be taken to several local shows before starting his serious show career. He may be required to walk up and down the ring with another Poodle who is running him close. This is quite a test, for he must not walk too close to the other dog and upset him, or pull on his leash, throwing his front legs out of the straight, in his efforts to get at him. To familiarize your Poodle to this situation, ask your friends to bring their dogs to your house or yard, and practice walking your Poodle with a dog he does not know.

He must also learn to accept sudden noises while in the ring. For instance, the sound system may often blare, or a table may fall to the ground with a clatter, or a burst of clapping and cheering may be heard in the next ring. If your Poodle flinches, perhaps cowers down and drops his tail, he will almost certainly lose marks for temperament. Therefore, such noises should be imitated while he is being trained. Often a phonograph or radio turned to full volume can be employed, or else friends may again be enlisted to bang tin trays or saucepan lids – in fact, anything to get him used to sudden loud noises.

Top quality show dogs must be trained to perfection. These three Miniatures are posing completely immobile, awaiting the next command.

The Miniature Poodle awaiting his call to enter the show ring, with two of his progeny in the background. By the time the pups are fully grown, they will be fairly familiar with the ring and at ease in strange situations.

BARBARA LOCKWOOD

But perhaps the most important of all is that he must learn to be at one with you, his handler. He must keep his eye on you all the time he is in the ring, and he must learn to respond to the softest spoken word, or the slightest twitch of the leash. Much of this attention can be inculcated in him by the offering of very small tidbits, and he will anticipate these and watch carefully for them. But not all of it can come through greediness or love of treats – much of it must be the result of his desire to please you, his delight in putting into practice all that he has learned for weeks beforehand, and, perhaps for the greatest reason of all, that showing has been bred into him for many generations and that these show traits spring into being when he feels the excitement and tension of the ring. If this is the case, you are lucky, because your Poodle will take to showing as a duck takes to water.

Training Yourself

You will need to train yourself, too. It is possible that you may be nervous, but you must not allow your nerves and self-consciousness to be passed to your Poodle. It is very easy for this feeling to pass down the leash! You must encourage him, you must keep his attention on you all the time, you must know exactly what you want him to do every moment of the time, both while training and at the actual show. You must not let his attention wander. And, incidentally, if you constantly concentrate on him, you will find that you have no time to be nervous yourself.

105

An early exercise which will help prepare the puppy for show, is to stand him on a table. The hindquarters should be well stretched back, tail up, front legs straight and parallel, and head erect. This white Toy is Babette of Pebble Lane. She is 8½ inches high, 2 years old, and in Royal Dutch clip. She is owned by Mrs. Edna Schepps of New York.

In Pixiecroft Minuteman we see the perfect Poodle eye. Dark, oval-shaped and alert, it typifies all that is best in the Poodle. Not only is Minuteman beautiful, but he is an excellent sire, producing many top-winning puppies.
Owned by Pixiecroft Kennels of New York.

Pixiecroft Daisy Mae has the short-backed, square look so desirable in the modern Poodle. She is well angulated. In one of the largest dog shows in the Eastern United States, the Westbury in 1967, Daisy Mae sailed through to Best of Winners. This is the type of Poodle we would all like to own.

There must be complete oneness between you and your Poodle. He will expect you to behave as you always have behaved while training him; he will expect you to lead him as you always have lead him, and any sign of uncertainty on your part will immediately unnerve him. If he is a good upstanding type of Poodle with a steady temperament, he should go into the ring almost demanding that Blue Ribbon simply because he knows his job.

American Shows

Dog shows in America and England follow very much the same pattern in the final awards, but differ somewhat in the earlier procedure. In America, all shows where championship points are on award must be held under the rules laid down by the American Kennel Club which takes over the responsibility of licensing the judges and the chief official who sponsors or manages the show, and who also keep records of all the points and awards which are given at every show. The sponsor of a show is either an all-breed dog club or a club interested in a special breed.

Often "Specialty Shows" are held which are restricted to a special breed – for instance, many of the state Poodle clubs run their own specialty. Sometimes a show is benched, which means that the dog must occupy a three-sided pen and remain there for the day, while at an unbenched show a dog need only stay at the show long enough to attend the classes in which he is entered. Points are awarded to the winning dogs based on the number of dogs actually entered and attending the show.

To become a Champion a dog must win a minimum of fifteen points under at least three different judges. Also, he must win a minimum of three points in each of two shows under different judges. The maximum number of points in any show is five. So it will be seen from this that a dog or bitch awarded the title of Champion really does face higher than average competition to win this honor.

All male dogs working for championship points must be entered in one of the five regular classes, and these are Puppy Class (for puppies from six months to one year); Novice Class, which is for dogs that have not won three First Prizes in Novice Classes, none in other classes (except Puppy), nor have gained any Championship points; Bred by Exhibitor Class, for dogs owned wholly or partly by the breeder, shown by him or members of his family, and which are not yet Champions; American-Bred Class, which is for dogs born in the United States, resulting from a mating which took place in the United States of America. And then finally there is the Open Class, which is open to any dog. This Class may be divided by height, weight or color. Precisely similar classes are scheduled for bitches. Ribbons are awarded for the winners of each of these classes, blue for first, red for second, yellow for third, and white for fourth. Champions *may* compete in the Puppy Classes and the Open Classes, but usually they are entered in the Specials Only Class.

Now the winners of each sex of each of the five foregoing classes compete against each other for the title of Winner's Dog and Winner's Bitch, for which they receive a Purple Ribbon, while both the Reserve Winner's Dog and Bitch receive Purple and White Ribbons. The Winner's Dog and the Winner's Bitch then compete against each other for the title of Best of Winners who receives a Blue and White Ribbon.

So this dog or bitch is now the best of his particular breed at the show, and the next move is for him to meet all the other Bests of Breed of his particular Group, and for this award he has to compete against the Specials Only (which are already Champions) and also the winners of the non-regular classes such as Local Class, Veteran Class, and so forth. So this dog really does face very high competition, and he will be trying to win the award of Winner of his special group and receive a Blue Rosette, There are six Groups: Sporting, Hound, Working, Terrier, Toy and Non-Sporting. The winners of each of these groups finally compete against each other for the supreme award of Best in Show, and win the coveted Red, White and Blue Rosette, or else a Rosette in the colors of the Kennel Club. He or she receives the points that count towards the Championship at the time of winning either Winner's Dog or Winner's Bitch.

It will readily be understood that it is a great feat to be a Group Show Winner and Best In Show.

English Shows

In the English show ring the procedure is exactly the same from the Best of Breed up to Best in Show. All Bests of Breed compete against each other in their respective Groups, and then the winner of all the six groups is judged Best in Show. The designations of the group

This fine Miniature Poodle being shown in England, shows a correct expression, dense, profuse coat, and jet-black pigmentation. Pigmentation is particularly important in white dogs, as there is a tendency for the eye rims, nose, or lips to be pale in color, which is undesirable.

SALLY ANNE THOMPSON

There is a great deal to be done readying a Poodle for a show. When away from the ring, a show dog like Champion Mike-Mar's Dream Come True, a 2½ year old Toy male, must have his topknot protected by cellophane. The oil on his coat keeps the ends from fraying. It will be bathed away just before the show.

TOM CARAVAGLIA

are slightly different for they are Hound, Terrier, Toy, Gun dog, Working and Utility. The classes which precede the award of Best of Breed are many and varied. These may be Puppy, Maiden, Novice, Graduate, Limit and many others, with finally the Open Class. All these classes are based on a handicapping system, and entry in them is in nearly all cases dependent on how many first Prizes have been won by the relevant dog. Ribbons are not usually awarded at English Shows, but colored cards are given for special awards and quite often rosettes, especially to Best of Breed winners.

The System for granting Championship status is quite different, and not based on a points system. A dog must win three challenge certificates under three different judges before he can become a champion. A challenge certificate is awarded to the best of each sex in every breed scheduled at a particular championship show. This means, of course, that the dog or bitch has to have beaten all others of his or her sex at the show, and when there are perhaps over two hundred Miniature Poodles entered, as was the case at Cruft's, this takes a tremendous lot of doing.

Dog shows provide a great deal of enjoyment. It is extremely interesting to watch the judging at a large show and follow it through its logical conclusion to Best in Show. It is a good idea, though, to have an idea of the procedure beforehand since, for the first time, it can be a confusing and bewildering set-up. Most Dog Shows are held in the open air in the summer, and providing the weather is good, this is ideal. The dogs can be freer, there is much more room, and a general air of friendliness prevails. The whole of dogdom seems to be on holiday. There are booths and stands where refreshments may be obtained, licensed bars, and traveling shops for the sale of dog foods and dog requisites. In the winter time, shows are usually held in public halls throughout the country, and though very friendly affairs, they do not offer the same degree of comfort and relaxation.

Pre-Show Preparation

If you plan to show your Poodle, and do not wish to employ the services of a professional handler, there are quite a lot of plans to be made well in advance, including a traveling case with brushes, combs, and all the other necessary toilet articles; food for your Poodle and yourself, a rug for his bench, the schedule of the show, and your various passes. You will need to know the route to the show ground or hall and that your automobile has sufficient gasoline. Allow plenty of time, for a rush at the last minute will fuss you, and this will be transmitted to your Poodle then neither of you will put on a good show!

As well as training your Poodle, you will need to train yourself. You must practice, practice, practice, until you are very sure of yourself and know exactly what to do. CREDIT: SALLY ANNE THOMPSON

Your First Show

When you arrive at the show your first job is to check with the veterinarian and then settle your Poodle comfortably on his bench. Next check the entries, then locate the judging ring, and finally settle yourself. It is very important when getting into the show and at the time of entering your classes, that you take particular care of your Poodle. This is a time when he may very easily be frightened. There are a lot of people milling about and a lot of feet! So if your Poodle is small enough to pick up, you would be wise to do so. At these times he can so easily be stepped on, or flurried, or, in the excitement of the moment, set on by another dog. It is important that he should arrive in the ring calm and unhurried, ready to make the most of himself.

As soon as you are in the judging ring, (and get in as early as you can), let your Poodle loosen up by walking him smartly up and down. Make a lot of fuss over him, and convey to him the idea that there is fun ahead. Let him frisk about a little if he wishes to, but be ready to bring him immediately to the show stance when the judge intimates that he is ready to start judging.

Ringcraft

It is an advantage to go into the ring as light as possible. One does see the exhibitor who puffs into the ring with the largest possible handbag, a brush and a comb, a squeaky toy for the Poodle, a scarf, a pair of gloves, and the schedule, and a large container of tidbits. Such an exhibitor usually manages to drop all these items at one point or another, even the dog's leash, and needless to say, the outcome of these efforts at showing are not very encouraging. Just a brush *or* a comb is all you will need, for it can be tucked in a pocket so much the better, as this will leave both hands free for controlling your Poodle.

Watch the judge carefully. If you let your attention wander you may miss his signal to call you in among the winners. Also keep your Poodle's attention on the judge because you never know when he may not cast an eye over the exhibits for a suitable candidate for that first prize.

If you win, remember to make much of your Poodle, never forgetting that you could not have done it without him! If you have been just missed out on first prize, remember to congratulate the winner, however disappointed you may feel.

There is nothing so exciting as winning your first ribbon. All the hard work, the exhausting training, the pre-show nerves are forgotten, and you and your Poodle are on top of the world. Your thoughts fly to even higher honors – perhaps one day that Best in Show award? Why not! If you are really single-minded and ambitious, you and your Poodle will get there – and there is nothing in the world quite like it!

TOM CARAVAGLIA

American Champion Jacques is 24 inches of Standard Poodle, and even in a sporting clip every inch a winner. He is 10 years old, but his appearance belies his years. Most Poodles are long-lived and retain their vigor. Owned by Mrs. Arnold Kaplan of New York.

Because we see so many of them in the city, we tend to think of Poodles as urban dogs only. Acutally, a Poodle can adjust to almost any situation and be at home anywhere.

IX The Obedient Poodle

Apart from general house manners, the Poodle should also apply himself to a certain amount of obedience training. He is extremely intelligent but even so, his intellect needs fostering and developing and the great thing in his favor is that he loves to learn.

Poodle ABC's

Training gradually opens up a new life for the young Poodle because it brings him into close companionship with his owner. The owner also benefits because he will find he has been able to achieve communication with a "dumb" animal, and together they can "talk." Indeed, it is possible to hold quite long conversations with a Poodle; admittedly it is one-sided, but at least it proves that the well-trained Poodle understands what is said to him, and his response, though it cannot be verbal, will manifest itself in quick responsive action to the spoken word. These words must be simple words of one syllable at first, and then gradually they can be built up into quite an extensive vocabulary of two or three syllable words, and then sentences of several words. He will learn to understand words as well as the average child of four years, provided he is carefully and patiently taught.

Primarily we are going to deal with a basic vocabulary of twelve words. These will be useful in the home; although some of these words are also employed in obedience training. The words dealt with here are simply suggestions; they may not all fit in with your own circumstances, and so you may have to work out your own twelve words. It is very exciting when your Poodle begins to understand the meaning of more and more words as his comprehension develops. In fact, there will come a time when words will have to be spelled if the Poodle is not to know what your are saying. And even spelling is not beyond his intelligence in due course!

He must be taught one word at a time, and not taken on to another word until he has completely mastered the first one. The training period for a specific word should last no longer than five or ten minutes at a time. The training must be kept as interesting as possible, and the dog must never be allowed to regard the period as boring, or even worse, frightening. Let him know that the training session will always end with something he enjoys, such as a scamper with a ball, or some special treat to which he is partial.

Work out in advance your schedule of twelve basic words which you intend to teach him. Suggested words are "Good dog", "No", "Heel", "Halt", or "Stop", "Sit", "Down", "Stay", "Come", "Fetch", "Drop", "Over", "Friend", "Foe". It will be seen that all these words, with the exception of "over", are monosyllables, and they should be given as definite, sharp, clipped commands. They are really the Poodle's ABC, and on to these basic commands can be built interesting sentences. But pick your own vocabulary and start training your Poodle puppy as soon as possible. You will find it fascinating to watch him collect more and more words as the capacity of his brain expands.

Now for his vocabulary of words and the actions that he must learn to connect with them:

1. *"Good dog."* These are almost the first words he will have heard in puppyhood; they indicate that he has behaved properly and pleased you with his action. Equally, the words "Bad" or "Naughty" will show him that he has failed to please you. But after these last words he must be quickly forgiven and not left in disgrace for long. Most Poodles are very sensitive and become

Training sessions should be short. Teach one command at a time and do not go on to another until he has completely mastered the first. This Poodle is learning to "shake hands". He should be taught to extend the right paw.

"Good dog!" It is important that you tell a Poodle when he has behaved properly and you are pleased with his actions. "Beg!" should be taught only to an older dog with a strong back. Hold something of interest above his head and help balance him with the lead.

"Heel!" As he walks alongside you, encourage him with your voice, control him with the lead, and pat your thigh to help him maintain the correct position alongside you.

easily discouraged. Make your point, then quickly forgive.

2. "*No!*" Another basic command that he will have learned in puppyhood, but which is useful also when learning the more complicated commands, and reacts incorrectly. If he does not obey a command which he knows perfectly well, or shows stupidity, then a sharp "No!" will bring him briskly to the point, especially if a severe tone of voice is used. All dogs like to please, and should be praised unstintingly when they do the right thing, just as they must be stopped by a sharp word as soon as they do the wrong thing.

3. "*Heel.*" To carry out this command, your Poodle should walk at a steady pace on your left side. First, clip on his leash and walk him short distances, keeping the leash short, so that his head is close to your leg. While you are walking him, say "Heel" every second or so in a sharp voice, accompanied by a brisk twitch on the leash. You should hold the leash in your right hand, and then with the leash passing across you, control it with your left hand. It must always be jerked in the direction you wish the Poodle to proceed. For instance, jerk forward when you start him off walking to heel, and jerk it back when you want him to stop. Never jerk the lead upwards as this conveys nothing.

After several days of practice he will have learned the meaning of the word, and will need no jerks from the lead. Try him off the leash. He will most probably continue to walk close to your left leg because a habit has been formed connected with the word "Heel." If by any chance he wanders away, immediately put him on the leash again and give him a few more lessons.

4. "*Halt*" or "*Stop.*" This follows heeling. As you give the command, bring yourself to a sudden stop with your feet together, at the same time jerking the leash backwards to check him. This is one of the first commands he must learn before crossing the highway.

5. "*Sit.*" Having taught your Poodle to heel on your left side, and to stop, teach him to sit. Bend forward, and with your right hand raise his muzzle; at the same time press his hindquarters down with your left hand, saying "Sit" in a sharp tone of voice. Make him sit until you are ready to release him.

6. "*Down.*" This must not be confused with the command "Sit," for now you will want him to lie down. It is usually a follow on to the sitting position, but not always so. It can also be taught from the standing position. Gently pull his front legs forward, and press his rear downwards, saying, "Down," all the time. This is a more

difficult command as, unless actually sleeping, dogs prefer the more alert position of sitting. But make sure that he stays down until you want him to do something else and give him the appropriate command. But at first make the periods "down" very short, possibly only a second or two, and then lengthen the time as he learns control.

7. *"Stay."* This, too, should be used in conjunction with either "Sit" or "Down." Here the command should be long drawn out, not sharp, and the vowel sound should be long – "Sta-a-ay" – and you should utter it while you back away for a few paces, with your arm stretched palm downwards, fingertips towards him. His natural reaction will be to follow you, so don't try his control too far to begin with, but the distance that you back away can be increased every day. Finally you should be able to turn your back on him and walk smartly away, knowing that he will not dream of moving until you give the word. You should even be able to disappear from sight, and still know he will stay. The usual thing that happens during this lesson is for the dog to "grovel" along the ground. He will not actually get up and walk towards you, but will steal along knowing that he should not! Go straight back to him, tell him to "Sit" or "Down", and then say "Sta-a-ay" several times, rapping his nose with your finger. This command is especially useful if you take your Poodle shopping and wish him to wait outside the shop for you, and, of course, equally useful in many other circumstances.

8. *"Come."* Whenever you wish him to proceed, either to start walking to heel, or from the sitting or down position, give a sharp jerk to the leash forwards, and say smartly "Come." You can also elaborate this command by using it to call him to you from a distance.

By now you have a string of words giving a sequence of movements. You will be able to give your Poodle a training period of at least ten minutes, during which he should be able to carry out as many as five definite exercises, not only in the order taught, but in any order you wish.

9. *"Fetch."* This is reasonably easy because all Poodles love to retrieve. The difficulty lies in getting the Poodle to bring the object back, and not just run away with it as a game. To start, have your Poodle on leash in the "Sit" position on your left side. Throw a ball, or a dumbbell or even a small block of wood, a few yards ahead

"Sit" is combined with "Heel," so that each time you stop while he is at heel he will sit alongside you in this position. At the command "Heel!" he will step out with you.

"Stay!" Here the command is being used in conjunction with "Sit." On the command of "Stay!" he must remain where he is even when you disappear from sight.

"Come!" On command the Poodle should arise and advance toward his trainer to either sit in front, on command, or else walk around behind his trainer and take up his position at "Heel!", i.e., close by the left leg of the trainer.

of you. He will probably try to rush after it, but jerk his collar back, and then after a second say, "Fetch," releasing your hold on his collar and giving him a push forward. As soon as he has picked up the object, smartly call him to "come". It may take quite some time before he can learn that there are two parts to this exercise, and "fetching" is of no use unless he "comes" back to you. Make a tremendous fuss over him when he fetches correctly.

10. "*Drop*." This is a continuation of the last lesson, for it is quite maddening if a dog hangs on to an object, obstinately refusing to give it to you. So having thrown the object, and induced him to wait for your commands "Fetch" and "Come," let him approach you, and then when he is standing in front of you say, "Sit," and then "Drop." At first he won't know why he should give up his prize, but persevere by forcing him to give it up, gradually instilling into his mind that when you place your fingers on the object and say, "Drop," he is to let go. Praise him extravagantly when he does drop it because he wants to hang on more than anything else, and it is a great step forward in his control when he relinquishes anything voluntarily. He should then, at the command, "Heel," pass behind you and come to sit closely by your left leg, waiting for the next throw.

These last commands have endless uses, for you can teach your Poodle to fetch your slippers, his own collar and leash, the morning paper, the letters, and he will soon become a handy fellow to have around. But a word of warning – when he is being trained he must carry out the commands and accompanying actions in strict rotation until he has really learned them as a routine. Only when you are sure that he is "word perfect" will you be able to give the commands out of sequence,

11. "*Over*." This is a command which applies specifically to crossing highways. However, it is of equal importance with other words, for the Poodle who is completely obedient when out on the highway, has a better chance of living to old age. To train him to cross the highway immediately on command, he must have approached the crossing at your side at "Heel." He should then "Sit" at your side on the edge of the sidewalk, and on your command of "Over" (or if you prefer the sharper word, "Go"), he should cross the highway immediately, keeping close to your left side.

12. "*Friend*" or "*Foe*." The command "Friend" is one which will often prove useful. It is not a word that should be used sharply;

he should learn to recognize it when it is said in a soft, and almost confidential tone of voice. If he barks at the approach of someone to your house (and every Poodle *should* bark until he finds out whether the caller is friendly or not), he should be told he is a "good dog" and then told, "Friend" (if this is the case), and a restraining hand should be held around his muzzle. If he continues to bark, sharply tell him, "No," and make sure that he stops, because needless barking can be extremely irritating both to yourself, your neighbors, and particularly to the friendly caller who cannot hear himself speak for the noise that is going on. You may prefer to use the word, "Quiet," but whatever restraining word is used, he must also be taught, "Friend," as this provides the reason to cease the barking.

"Foe" is a word not often used, but since it could be useful in an emergency, especially if you live alone or in an isolated place, it should have a special meaning for your dog. If your Poodle makes a

"Fetch" is reasonably easy because all Poodles love to retrieve. Make a tremendous fuss over him when he fetches correctly.

One thing a Poodle should learn early is not to rear up on you. It's fun when you're in playclothes, but he doesn't know the difference when you're wearing your Sunday best. Either tread gently on his back toes, or raise your knee so that he bumps against it, and say "No!" sharply.

lot of noise, appearing difficult to restrain, it will serve as a crime deterrent. Keep your hand on his collar, and at the same time say, "Foe," and add other phrases like, "Get him!" or, "At him." The Poodle will then appear a great deal fiercer than he really is, and no intruder will care to lay himself open to his attack.

So there will be quite a lot of homework for your Poodle before he masters his basic ABC. But there is no doubt that if you take a lot of trouble, are patient and really persevere, you will soon have a Poodle of whom you can be immensely proud, one who will be the envy of your neighbors.

Obedience Trials

The foregoing applies to simple obedience training, but Poodles have proved themselves highly efficient in the wider field of obedience trials. Some dogs do well in both show classes and obedience classes, but not all of them. The reason for this is that behavior in the show ring is just the opposite to that required in obedience trials.

For instance, the show dog must stand completely still while the judge is making his examination, but in obedience work, the dog must sit close to his owner's left leg when he is not carrying out an exercise. The show dog must not walk strictly at heel, but should walk ahead, covering the ground at the end of his lead.

There is a tremendous amount to learn before the dog is a really first class obedience trained dog, although, of course, there are classes for the beginner that do not demand too much skill. In the open classes, the training is complicated and quite difficult.

There is not enough space in a book that covers all aspects of the Poodle to deal with obedience training in detail. The best way to learn the ins and outs of obedience work is to join a regular training class where both you and your Poodle will be taught what to do.

Many obedience trials are held in conjunction with dog shows, and quite a few Poodles have obtained top honors in both spheres in America and England. A Poodle able to cover both aspects of such training, since the methods are so completely different, is a most intelligent and clever dog, and one to be greatly valued.

By introducing a Poodle to other animals at an early age, he will learn to accept them without question. Cats, chickens, rabbits, squirrels – he should meet them all and learn that they are his friends.

SALLY ANNE THOMPSON

A well-balanced diet is essential to keep your Poodle in vigorous good health.

X Feeding the Poodle

Remember when you plan your dog's diet that feeding time is the most important time of his day. If he is a normal healthy dog, his mealtimes will be a longingly anticipated joy. He cannot tell you his likes and dislikes, nor does he take into account what is good for him. It is up to you to use your knowledge to give him the right food, in the right amount, at the right time of day.

Some owners prefer to plan their dog's diet and prepare the food themselves; others rely on packaged dog foods. First let us consider some general feeding procedures and then examine both methods.

Quality

To begin with, the food must be of good quality. Anything less will not keep him in good health and fine coat. It is false economy to feed scraps and offal as substitutes for good nutritious dog food. Certainly, as a change, organ meat like liver, heart, kidney and tripe may be given and they will be much appreciated, but as a regular diet such things do not provide the needed body-building nutriments.

The preparation of meat, if you use fresh meat in the diet, is especially important, for it should not be overcooked. Often one hears of the breeder who keeps a stock-pot going for the dog, and in it the meat is boiled until some of the essential nutriments have been destroyed by heat. This is not good for the Poodle who is shown, the busy stud dog or the brood bitch; nor does it really satisfy the companion dog who admittedly does not lead their energetic life.

Temperature

Food and drink should always be served at the right temperature, neither too cold nor too hot. Food taken from the refrigerator and fed at once may cause gastritis or some other digestive trouble. On the other hand, a meal that is too hot will upset the dog and put him off his feed. Dogs will not eat food as hot as the human palate can tolerate. The ideal temperature is slightly tepid. Drinks for puppies should be given at an approximate temperature of 70°.

Cleanliness

This is another important point. Bowls should be kept scrupulously clean, and washed thoroughly after each meal. Putting the food into the dish still on the floor from the last meal, and sometimes even on top of the food that is left, is a dreadful habit. It should not be the last surprising if the dog has no appetite, or suffers from digestive upsets.

Then again, the Poodle must be comfortable in his eating place. He should not be expected to eat in a chilling wind, or in burning sun, or in the rain. His dining place should be cool, dry and clean. He should have ample opportunity to relieve himself before eating, but he should not be shut out for so long a period before mealtime that he feels neglected and upset before he starts to eat.

Time and Place

A regular timetable should be adhered to. Meals are of great importance to all dogs. They have a biologically built-in clock which tells them when dinner ought to be ready. Therefore, if his meal is late your dog is going to fret, and unless there is some good reason for the delay, do not cause him anxiety.

Poodles with varying dispositions need different handling when it comes to feeding. A shy and nervous dog will often do more justice to his meal if he is fed alone. The fear of a dog with a more dominant personality, eating in the same place, may completely upset him. On the other hand, a "choosey" and uninterested feeder may feed much better if another dog, or even a cat, is in the same room, because natural protection of his property will spur him on.

Balance and Variety

There is no doubt that if you are to feed your dog to his full physical and mental growth, and compound his diet yourself, a great deal of time, trouble, forethought, patience and even psychology must be employed. When planning the Poodle's diet, two points must be considered: food must be of the highest quality, and the diet must be balanced.

Feeding foodstuffs of high quality is in itself an economy, for good health will result, obviating the expense of extra tonics and appetizers and minimizing veterinary bills. A balanced diet must contain the correct proportions of Proteins, Carbohydrates and Fats. Proteins are supplied by meat, fish, eggs, and cheese. Carbohydrates by cereals, biscuits, bread, and potatoes. The Fat proportion is found in a certain amount of fatty meat, fish oils, and the butter content of milk or the fat in margarine. Since milk also contains protein and minerals, it often has a place in many diets. Variety in the diet will help to keep the Poodle's appetite keen, but it is really not essential as those who feed the same prepared food day after day can attest.

How Much Food

If you feed fresh meat, to gauge the amount of food required, feed half an ounce of good quality lean meat to every pound of body weight. Thus a dog weighing 14 to 16 pounds will need seven to eight ounces of meat daily. But to this *must* be added dog meal or other supplements.

If a dog who is normally a good feeder refuses his food, or appears to have little enthusiasm for it, his temperature should be taken immediately, as this may well be the first symptom of some disease or infection. If you are perceptive enough to notice this sign right at the beginning, you may prevent more serious trouble.

SALLY ANNE THOMPSON

This is a magnificent study of a white Miniature Poodle showing the correct shape of eye, and excellent black pigment of nose and lips. The hairdo is correct for the show ring. This dog has the elegant, dignified expression which is so typical in the best specimens of this breed. The diet for show dogs like this is carefully regulated to provide the correct proportions of protein, carbohydrate and fat. Quantities are also regulated to avoid the dog's becoming either too lean or too heavy.

Poodles by the Dozen

The authors used to feed twelve Show Poodles at the same time at a long low table which stood about ten inches high. Each Poodle had a groove inset to fit his dish, and at the top was a bar to which was fixed his own name plate. The Poodles when called into their "dining-room" would immediately take up their correct positions side by side; they never made a mistake. Visitors to the kennels were highly amused and very much surprised, asking if the Poodles could read! It was simply routine. It would have presented a problem if for some reason a Poodle had to take another place. They definitely felt relaxed and comfortable in the spot they knew as their own, and because of this and competition from their immediate neigbor, appetites were keen and there were no leftovers. It was a rare occurrence to hear any growls or rude remarks from the "diners."

The real purpose of this feeding routine was a show training exercise, for the Poodles learned to stretch their necks and hold their heads high; nor did they throw out their shoulders by dropping their heads to feed from ground level. This arrangement did much to account for the splendid head carriage and straight fronts of the famed prize winning Rothara Poodles.

Main Meal

This can be fed at any time convenient after noon. In hot weather it is best given in the early evening: Two or three handfuls of commercial kibble,one tablespoonful of raw, finely grated carrot, one tablespoonful chopped watercress and/or parsley,1½ to 2½ pounds of fresh meat, part of which can be fish, or cottage cheese. A small cupful of boiling broth can be used to mix the meat and kibble, and one teaspoonful each of pure olive oil and halibut liver oil may be added just before feeding. The oil will stick to the sides of the bowl and be wasted if it is added during the mixing.

Bedtime – Cupful of half and half milk and water, large dog biscuit to chew and help keep the teeth clean, a cube of well-boiled liver or a large beef bone also for his "tooth brush".

Variations – Give fish instead of meat occasionally, and add a couple of egg yolks (discard the white if fed raw). Organ meat can also make up half the meat ration on occasion. Do not cut the meat up too small. Large chunks weighing two or three ounces are about right and give exercise to jaws and teeth, provoking saliva and assisting the digestion. Ground meat, strangely enough, does not digest as easily as meat in chunks.

Appetite

A well exercised dog in good health will eat heartily although the amount he might eat will vary a little, as it does with humans, due to the rate of metabolism and variables like size, age and temperament. A lively energetic dog will always consume more than one with a quiet, placid disposition, although both may be in perfect health. Any healthy dog will eat about one-third more than he needs for daily living, so always underfeed a little.

The Poodle is not as a rule a greedy feeder, although there are some notable exceptions – usually the ones that put on weight easily – and it is always a hard task to reduce their food intake. A dog's digestive processes take about nine hours (that is, the adult). It can easily be calculated the harm feeding and dainties does during this interval, just as it is harmful to give a child candy between meals. The fact that the dog *will* eat does not mean that he *should* eat and you must be severe with your family and friends if they offer him tasty morsels at table. In my estimation, sugar, particularly, is a great enemy of the dog and you must explain that these indulgences can shorten your pet's life.

If the dog's appetite is poor or erratic, check for worms, (tape or round) and note if the dog is constipated or if the bowel movement is irregular. Normally, stools are passed twice daily in an active animal and once in an older or less energetic one. A puppy may have five or six.

Some kennels practice the habit of a weekly fast day, and this is highly recommended by the natural health practitioners. However, it is not so easy with a house pet, although once the routine is established the dog seems to accept the day of abstinence without objection. The plan is to leave him for one day on water only, or if you feel it is less harsh, half and half milk and water with a small quantity of honey or Karo, particularly in winter when the fasting dog may feel chilled if he is deprived of all nourishment. Milk, of course, is food, Karo is glucose, a sugar, so if you give very much the dog is really not fasted.

Some feed a small meal of meat on the morning following the fast and the usual meal minus this portion of meat at the customary feeding time. Fasting is, of course, only practiced with adults, although a half day's fast is often beneficial to puppies at teething time when the digestion is disturbed. Purging is recommended at the conclusion of a long fast. For large puppies give a dessertspoonful of milk of magnesia and for adults a large tablespoonful or the same quantitity of mineral oil (liquid paraffin).

If your dog does not eat heartily following this routine it might be wise to take him to your veterinarian for a check up. The appetite really depends on a properly established rhythm and this should follow the one which nature herself planned for the dog in his wild state, when he would go forth to run and hunt, and having killed his prey would eat, then retire to sleep.

A wolf will eat a 20 pound meal and sleep two days, but sometimes he eats lemmings and other small rodents which do not glut him and he will continue hunting except for short rest intervals. Exercise should precede food, and sleep follow it. A dog will sometimes play with a companion, chew his bone or tease a toy after his meal, but sleep soon overcomes him as digestion gets under way and he should not be disturbed. His natural hours for rest and elimination are, approximately, from midnight to midday. So we like to feed the main meal between five and six p.m. Then the dog rests quietly during the evening, has his last exercise before midnight and is less drowsy during the early hours of the morning when he should be on duty as your watchdog. Again, with his rhythm working smoothly, he will be ready to exercise and eliminate at the first opportunity next morning. This program requires regular hours for feeding and exercising, the reward being a healthy pet who will live a long and happy life.

The last meal between five and six o'clock followed by a late evening walk, gives a puppy the opportunity to empty himself, making it easier for him to go through the night without an accident.

Commercial Foods

Nowadays, a tremendous amount of research goes into the production of dog foods. Tests for palatability, for growth of coat, for steady maintenance of condition – all with their supporting clinical studies – are carried out by many of the leading dog food manufacturers. Also vitamins and minerals and their corresponding values are exhaustively explored in laboratory tests, and then added to enrich many foodstuffs. So there is no reason why the modern dog should not have in his diet every possible ingredient that will enhance the condition of his body and coat, and also nourish his nervous system to aid in breeding puppies whose temperaments are steady and whose dispositions are pleasant.

An American authority on dog nutrition has stated that there are as many different diets for dogs as there are dogs. After all of the millions of dollars which have been spent on dog foods to make them complete in every nutritional respect, there are still those who ignore all of this research and insist on concocting their own mixtures. Probably no diet which the average dog owner can produce will be more nutritious, and by no means more complete or growth promoting, than the better grades of prepared foods for sale in almost all markets. Some are in cans (the more expensive kinds), some are ready to feed with the addition of only a small amount of water – 25% in contrast to 74% water in canned food. Some are dried in the form of meal or pellets.

For economy the last two are the best. Most of the brands are deficient however in fat and so fat should be added – 10% to 15% of the ration. Any edible fat will do, whether it be margarine made from vegetable oils, ground-up trimmings from the butcher's fat barrel or what have you – frying pan fat, fat removed from the top of a soup kettle, dogs love and digest it all.

We have no quarrel with those who want to waste time and money buying fresh meat, feeding eggs, milk and human foods to their dogs. But we do know that for kennel dogs, such a procedure is a great waste of time and money, and even a house pet will thrive on prepared foods.

It may be as difficult for dog owners, steeped in the old tradition of feeding so prevalent a generation ago, to change and adopt scientifically demonstrated facts about feeding, as it is for some persons to change their religions. "Time makes ancient good uncouth."

We know that dogs do not need fresh muscle meat, they can live equally well on many other things such as fish or whale (which, of course, is mammalian). They can also live on animal proteins which have been dried. Dogs can not digest egg white; the raw yolk *is* digestible but it costs almost as much to feed one egg as it costs for an entire day's commercial ration. Dogs can digest starch if it is baked, and sweets also, and lots of other items. Some even relish various kinds of fruit.

To make feeding your pet Poodle or kennel of Poodles as easy and economical as any method we can conceive, use high grade

Children love the cuddly Poodle. Let the child feed the dog regularly. He will appreciate the responsibility, and the dog will become more attached to his little master.

dry dog meal or kibble and add extra fat. This is good for every dog from weaning through old age.

Of course, if your dog is a home companion, and you can't resist his pleading eyes, you can also treat him to a hard dog biscuit to help keep his teeth clean and his breath sweet.

What Not To Feed

Do not feed fish, pork or chicken bones; they can splinter and choke the dog or jagged points can penetrate the alimentary canal. Beef rib, shin or marrow bones, or ham hocks are fine. They also make good playthings, and rib bones, in particular, are good teethers and "toothbrushes".

Avoid spicy foods, fried foods and sweets. No candy, no cookies, no cake. They spoil him for other foods, filling him up with useless calories and dulling his appetite for more nourishing food. Besides, as with children, sweets are hard on the teeth, inviting cavities. We are not by any means referring to the special prepared dog "candies" and "sweets" which are made without sugar and are highly nutritious.

Don't pass your pet any bones or scraps from the table at least not while you're eating, and always place them in his own bowl in its usual spot. Feed the dog before you eat, or, if his regular feeding time comes later, keep him out of the dining area until the table is cleared. There is nothing more disconcerting to a guest than to watch the family dog eye longingly every mouthful he puts into his mouth.

Water

Your dog should be offered fresh, cool water about three times a day. Do not allow him water within an hour before or an hour after feeding, nor immediately after violent exercise. Aside from these times, you can keep fresh water available constantly if you wish. But it is better perhaps to set down a fresh bowl for him briefly several times a day. Then you are always sure that it's cool and uncontaminated. The average dog requires about 8 ounces of water a day.

Correct Weight

It is important to keep a weekly check on the weight of your Poodle. He should be placed on the scales on the same day of each week, at approximately the same time, when similar conditions prevail. For instance, it is better to weigh him in the morning before he has had a meal, and preferably after his bowels have moved. The weights should be noted down with other relevant records. Appropriate action should then be taken if he has lost or gained too much weight. A small chart will help you to see at a glance if there is any significant deviation from the norm week by week.

As a rough guide, the height of a young Miniature or Toy Poodle in inches very nearly corresponds to his weight in pounds, although as the dog matures, his weight is inclined to exceed the comparative number of inches of his height by about 25%. Therefore, a young Miniature Poodle standing 14 inches at the shoulder should weigh approximately 14 pounds; this will increase to possibly 17 or 18 pounds as he grows older. A nine inch Toy Poodle should weigh around nine pounds or less. Obviously, this does not always work out as the Poodle may be a heavy-bodied type on very short legs, who may weigh a good 12 pounds and yet be only eight inches tall. But in the normal, well-balanced Poodle, it is a fairly reliable guide. This does not apply to the mature Standard for a dog 23 inches at the shoulder may weigh 50 pounds.

The Lactating Bitch

Everyone should know that the milk which a bitch produces for her puppies is copious, actually much more in proportion to her size than any world's record cow ever produced. Moreover the milk contains 10-12% fat where the cow's milk is about 3.5% to 4.0% fat.

The wild bitch which kills her own food for her puppies consumes food with at least 30% fat. What the lactating bitch requires is a goodly supply of fat in addition to the meal type dog food. Her diet can be 30% fat. If it is, she will not lose weight and her puppies will usually be plump and roly-poly.

Young Puppies

If the puppies are at all loose in their bowel movements, it is usually a sign that worming is necessary and it is safe to dose them from the age of six weeks onwards. If, on the other hand, the puppies are slightly constipated, a few drops of olive oil will remedy this condition. Large beef bones may now be given to help the puppies cut their teeth, or hard dog biscuits are relished. Many of these are nutritionally, and most worthwhile for chewing exercise.

Diet for Growing Youngsters (3–6 months)

At the age of three months a puppy can begin a special dry puppy food, moistened as directed and with some fat added, if necessary. This can constitute the dog's food for the rest of its life; but most likely, especially in the case of Toys, it will not. If it does, the dog will doubtless be far healthier than most pampered old Toys.

Diet for the Aging Poodle

If you examine the teeth of any elderly Toy Poodle or dog of any of the midget breeds, probably you will find its teeth loose or missing, or they may have been extracted by a veterinarian. The chief reason for this loss of teeth is first, the dog's diet has been inadequate because of pampering, and second the lack of anything hard to chew has permitted tartar to accumulate on the teeth close to the gums. The gums have receded, the teeth have become loose and at that point the dog cannot chew anything hard because of the pain he feels whenever he attempts it.

His breath becomes objectionable. Out come his teeth – poor little dog. He is the victim of his owners carelessness and thoughtlessness! What is the way to prevent this curse of his old age?

The remedy is foresight and proper feeding. Proper feeding consists of supplying the foods which are complete nutritionally. and keeping the teeth clean. Hard dog biscuits on which he can crunch will prevent tartar from forming. Soft rib bones will too, but they tend to be constipating. If biscuits do not remove the tartar have your veterinarian do it.

For his entire life, do not permit him to become spoiled. Keep him on the complete diet and keep him hungry. Remember that any dog will eat a third more than he needs every day, so feed him about two thirds of what you find he will eat. If he loses weight increase the amount of food slightly. Remember that goodies which you feed in response to his pleading must be counted as part of his diet. And goodies include milk, ice cream, and table scraps perhaps fed from your table. You know that most table scraps are not a complete diet or the elderly persons among your acquaintances would not be wearing dentures.

And remember too that fasting is not at all painful. It often pays to fast a dog for a day or two to encourage him to eat what you know is good for him. Any fat dog, midget or large, can live two months on only water, so don't feel you are being cruel if you have to fast your Poodle for a few days.

Special Foods for Invalid Dogs

For any Poodle who is slightly indisposed, or showing any sign of a temperature, complete starvation for at least 24 hours is useful.

After that, drinks of cold boiled water should be given at three hour intervals, until the temperature is again normal. Honey with water is excellent in the case of chills, or sudden slight sickness. Any solid food given at such a time will only irritate the Poodle's condition. At the first sign of sickness, the veterinarian should be called. He will prescribe the proper diet.

Nutrient Requirements

A great deal of work on dog nutrition is being done by governmental agencies. This work is not only investigatory but is also necessary because the government sets standards for pet food manufacturers. A summary of some of the findings of the Subcommittee on Canine Nutrition of the National Academy of Sciences condensed into chart form are given here.

You can almost hear this Standard Poodle saying to the Toy, "No, little fellow, no matter how much you eat you'll never grow as big as I am."

Table I will be of interest to those who would like to prepare their own mix, and for those who are curious as to just what goes into a commercial dog food. It is a breakdown of two different meal-type rations.

Table I
Meal-Type Rations for Dogs [1]
(Dry matter 91%)

Ingredient	Ration 1 %	Ration 2 %
Meat and bone meal, 55% protein	8.00	15.00
Fish meal, 60% protein	5.00	3.00
Soybean oil meal	12.00	—
Soybean grits	—	19.00
Wheat germ oil meal	8.00	5.00
Skim milk, dried	4.00	2.50
Cereal grains	51.23	—
Corn flakes	—	26.75
Wheat bran	4.00	—
Wheat flakes	—	26.70
Fat, edible	2.00	—
Bone meal, steamed	2.00	—
Brewers yeast, dried	2.00	0.50
Fermentation solubles, dried	1.00	—
Salt, iodized	0.50	0.25
Vitamin A & D feeding oil (2,250 IU of A, 400 IU of D per gm)	0.25	0.50
Riboflavin supplement [2]	—	0.80
Iron oxide	0.02	—

[1] While these rations have been used satisfactorily with some dogs, there is no assurance that all dogs will accept them readily.
[2] BY-500.

Table II lists a dog's requirements in terms of food components per pound of body weight. It is interesting to note that growing puppies (last column) require two or more times as much of each of these nutrients as do adult dogs.

Table II

Nutrient Requirements of Dogs [1]
(Amounts per pound of body weight per day)

	Weight of dog in pounds	Adult maintenance	Growing puppies
Energy (kcal) [2]	5	50	100
	10	42	84
	15	35	70
	30	32	64
		31	62
Protein-minimum (gm)		2.0	4.0
Carbohydrate-maximum (gm) [3]		0.4	7.2
Fat (gm)		0.6	1.2
Minerals:			
Calcium (mg)		120	240
Phosphorus (mg)		100	200
Iron (mg)		0.600	0.600
Copper (mg)		0.075	0.075
Cobalt (mg)		0.025	0.025
Sodium Chloride (mg)		170	240
Potassium (mg)		100	200
Magnesium (mg)		5	10
Manganese (mg)		0.050	0.100
Zinc (mg)		0.050	0.100
Iodine (mg)		0.015	0.030
Vitamins:			
Vitamin A (IU) [3]		45	90
Vitamin D (IU) [3]		3	9
Vitamin E (mg)		–	1
Vitamin B_{12} (mg)		0.0003	0.0006
Folic acid (mg)		0.002	0.004
Riboflavin (mg)		0.020	0.040
Pyridoxine (mg)		0.010	0.020
Pantothenic acid (mg)		0.023	0.045
Niacin (mg)		0.110	0.180
Choline (mg)		15	30

While the amount of food required by a dog varies, depending on such things as the dog's own metabolism, activity, environment, and so on, as we have previously noted the greatest difference will be found between the requirements of a growing dog and an adult. Table III gives the estimated daily food intake required by dogs of various sizes, broken down into *Requirements for Maintenance* – this covers the average non-working dog under normal conditions – and *Requirements for Growth* – these are the amounts of food required by a growing dog. While some adjustments in these amounts may be required for your own pet, they do serve as guidelines when estimating how much to feed your dog. An old dog will probably require less food than indicated here, while a pregnant or nursing bitch will require more.

Table II footnotes

[1] Symbols – gm = gram; mg = milligram; IU = International Unit.

[2] Values listed are for gross or calculated energy. Biologically available energy is ordinarily 75-85 per cent of the calculated.

[3] The values shown are based upon dry foods containing 91 and 28 per cent dry matter. Moisture has been included to indicate general level of composition rather than as a requirement. There is no evidence that carbohydrate as such is required, but since it occurs as a part of many dog-food ingredients, a maximum value has been suggested.

The 0.6 and 0.18 mg quantity of crystalline vitamin A is equal to 2000 and 600 IU, respectively. One mg vitamin A alcohol = 3,333 IU of vitamin A. One mg beta carotene = 1,667 IU of vitamin-A activity. For dogs carotene is approximately one-half as valuable as vitamin-A alcohol.

These amounts of pure vitamin D correspond to 120 and 40 IU per pound of feed.

Table III

Estimated daily Food Intakes Required by Dogs of Various Sizes

Weight of dog	Requirements for maintenance			
	Dry type foods [1]		Canned dog food [2]	
	Per lb body wt	Per dog	Per lb body wt	Per dog
lbs	lbs	lbs	lbs	lbs
5	0.040	0.20	0.120	0.60
10	0.033	0.33	0.101	1.01
15	0.028	0.42	0.085	1.27
20	0.027	0.54	0.081	1.60
30	0.025	0.75	0.077	2.30
50	0.025	1.25	0.075	3.74
70	0.025	1.75	0.075	5.23
110	0.024	2.64	0.074	8.22

Weight of dog	Requirements for growth			
	Dry type foods [1]		Canned dog food [2]	
	Per lb body wt	Per dog	Per lb body wt	Per dog
lbs	lbs	lbs	lbs	lbs
5	0.080	0.40	0.240	1.20
10	0.066	0.66	0.202	2.02
15	0.056	0.84	0.190	2.54
20	0.054	1.08	0.160	3.20
30	0.050	1.50	0.154	4.60
50	0.050	2.60	0.150	7.48
70	0.050	3.50	0.150	10.46
110	0.048	5.28	–	–

[1] Dry foods contain 6-12 per cent moisture. Calculations of the amounts of dry food required have been based on energy supplied by food containing 91 per cent dry matter, 76 per cent protein plus carbohydrate, 5 per cent fat and 10 per cent ash, fiber and other inert material. This supplies a calculated 1583 kcal per pound, of which it is estimated that 80 per cent or 1266 kcal are digestible.

[2] Calculated on the basis of 28 per cent dry matter and the same nutrient rations as in 1, with the total and available energy calculated as 490 and 415 (85 percent of the total) kcal per pound.

This is one way to keep them from getting dirty while they dry. It's not really practical, but it does make a nice picture.

XI Grooming and Shampooing

You will, by now, have been thinking about the care of your Poodle's coat, and, we hope, grooming him carefully every day with a gentle brush and comb even while a young puppy. But now his coat is growing thicker and longer, and you will probably be wondering which brushes and combs are really right for his coat.

Brush

There are various tools which are essential to good grooming, and there are other items which will help with coat maintenance but are not strictly necessary.

In the "must" category are brushes, combs, a hairdrier and nail-clippers. There are many brushes suitable for the Poodle. Nearly all brushes good for the human hair are good for the Poodle coat; conversely, many dog brushes are totally unsuited to the special requirements of the Poodle. Wire brushes or curry combs, regularly used for the terrier breeds, are far too harsh for the texture of the Poodle coat. Moreover, some of the brushes employed to groom many of the soft and silky-coated Toy breeds are just as unsuitable.

141

The coat of the Poodle should be thick, dense, and springy — not in any way soft and silky. Thus, any type of brush with whalebone bristles is suitable; such a brush will get right down to the roots of the hair. A pneumatic brush with nylon tufts bedded into the rubber cushion is also suitable. These can be purchased with a webbing strap across the back, but we have found that those with a handle are easier to use. A wire brush, or curry comb type of brush (were the wire claws are set in canvas with a metal back) should only be used if the Poodle's coat has become matted or "felted." Then the wire brush will be useful for "teasing" out those knots of tangled hair, but it is a desperate method for a desperate situation. The Poodle owner who really looks after his Poodle's coat will never let the coat get into this state! Brushes should be kept scrupulously clean and washed once a week, for a dirty brush will clog the hair and do more harm than good.

Comb

The selection of a suitable comb also requires thought. There are many on the market, and many are totally unsuitable for the Poodle. A metal comb is the best; it should be really wide toothed. A comb with the teeth spaced 3/16ths of an inch apart is by no means too wide for overall grooming, but a second comb is needed for the short areas, and this can have teeth spaced 1/16th of an inch apart. It is good economy to buy a comb of chromium plated brass for such combs will last a long time, will stand up to constant washing in detergent, and will have extremely strong prongs which do not buckle or bend. The less expensive steel comb with nickel-*plated* pins does not stand up to heavy usage, and when cleansed in detergent or disinfectant, its metal plating is inclined to peel off. The rough edges then catch in the Poodle's coat and do a great deal of damage. A very useful brass and chromium comb is one about seven inches long, half of which has the teeth widely spaced, and the other half closely spaced. There are many groomers, however, who prefer combs with handles.

Hairdrier

A hairdrier is an essential because a Poodle needs to be bathed fairly often if he is to always look smart and dapper. Unless he is to be sent to the grooming parlor for bathing – and this as a regular happening costs money – he will need to be put in the tub at home at fairly frequent intervals. To get a smart finish on the pet Poodle, a hand hairdrier helps tremendously, and, of course, with the show dog it is absolutely essential that he not be "rough dried" with a towel in the sun or in front of a fire. So if it is at all possible, an electric hairdrier should be obtained. There are several brands made especially for dogs, but those intended for humans are just as suitable, and can, if you wish, serve a dual purpose.

Nailclippers

Nailclippers are another necessary item; the "guillotine" type is better than the "nipper". The guillotine type has a hole into which the tip of the nail is inserted; a sharp blade then snips cleanly through the nail when the handles of the clippers are squeezed together. The nipper type is inclined to squash the nail before cutting through it, frequently causing sudden pain, but with the guillotine type no resistance is offered,

Clipping

The foregoing grooming tools are necessary for the day to day grooming and routine bathing of the Poodle who will, in addition, visit the beauty parlor for regular clipping. But if you wish to attend to all aspects of your Poodle's maintenance, including clipping, you will need more equipment.

There is no doubt that sending the Poodle to the beauty parlor every six weeks or so does cost money, and it is our aim in this and the following chapters to teach you how to shampoo, clip, trim and maintain your Poodle at home, and save yourself a lot of extra expense.

To embark on this most interesting side of Poodle ownership, you must equip yourself with additional tools, practice hard, and study every possible technique. We hope to show you how to carry out every stage of Poodle beauty treatment, for, beond doubt, the owner who is entirely responsible for the "chic" appearance of his Poodle will take tremendous pride in his results. Clipping is not too difficult; it is simply a matter of practice and soon the home clipped Poodle will take his place amongst the smartest of his fellows.

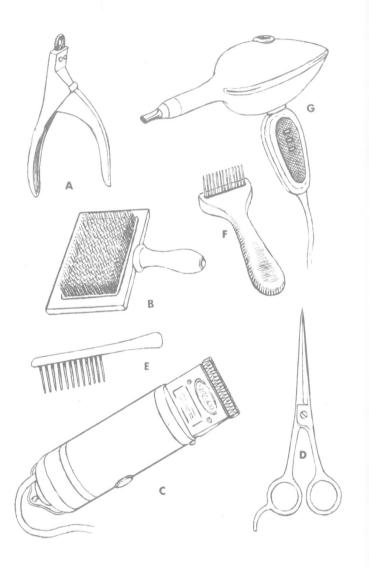

Poodle grooming equipment.

A. – Nail clipper.
B. – Wire brush.
C. – Clipper.

D. – Scissor.
E. – Comb.
F. – Rake.
G. – Cage blower.

Too, it may open up another avenue, for quite often the owner who who turns out his own Poodle to perfection will soon receive requests from other Poodle owners to undertake the regular grooming and clipping of their pets, and eventually their show dogs. In time, a profitable sideline can be built up.

The Clipper

So, the matter of clippers must be explored. There are many makes and designs on the market, and the choice may well rest on what you are prepared to pay. The manual type may be adequate to begin with, but they are difficult to manipulate as the clipper itself must be moved slowly while the hand manipulation of the blades must be done extremely quickly. There is a knack to this, but it takes time to learn. If it is financially possible, we strongly advise that an electric clipper be invested in right from the start. Those with an electric motor, as opposed to an agitator, are more efficient, but of course more expensive.

The more elaborate clipper usually has detachable heads onto which may be screwed or fitted varying types of blades, ranging from "coarse" (suitable for cutting down the long shaggy coat to a manageable length of approximately 1/2 to 3/4 of an inch), the medium blade (for the short-haired areas in the Lion Clip or Dutch Clip), the "close" blade (designed for clipping face, feet and tail), and a still finer blade intend for close clipping of areas for surgical work.

These clipper blades are usually known by a number, the coarse being a 5 mm or 7 mm, the medium, a 10 mm or 15 mm, while 30 mm is the close blade, and 40 mm the surgical type. Usually available are special Poodle blades intended principally for clipping the feet and toes, and these are generally 5/8ths or 7/8ths of an inch wide, with blades equal to the close type.

When choosing electric clippers bear in mind the question of weight, for a heavy clipper can be very tiring; one weighing approximately 1 1/4 pounds is the most comfortable. Vibration should also be considered, for obviously a machine with an electric motor is going to carry with it a certain amount of vibration and noise. Therefore, test several makes, and for the comfort of your Poodle try to choose the clipper with the least noise and vibration, but one that has a quick, sharp performance, and a blade easy to change.

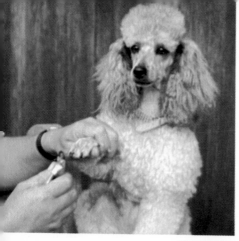

Hold the nails up to the light. The dark area in the center is the quick. Avoid cutting into it.

A rubber spray unit with a sprinkler head helps remove every last bit of soap.

How long does it take a Poodle's coat to grow? This Poodle, being sprayed with a tonic which promotes the growth of coat, will be able with proper care to grow a long coat suitable for shaping into the English Saddle clip for the show ring within six to eight months.

The clipper that is operated by an agitator instead of an electric motor is undoubtedly lighter in weight and less noisy, and causes far less vibration, but its cutting finish is not so professional. Practically all cutting blades are detachable, some more easily than others, and so the matter of regrinding does not present a problem.

Stand Drier

The hand hairdrier will probably suffice, but if you progress to coping with the toilet of several Poodles each day, you will undoubtedly want to invest in a more elaborate power drier or stand drier, which cuts the drying time of a normal Poodle from approximately 30 or 40 minutes to, say, 10 or 20 minutes. The power drier has various drying heats but it is a little heavy to hold if a number of Poodles are to be dried. The stand drier is easier in that it is adjustable in height and direction of nozzle, usually having two or more heat elements, and is moderately quiet in operation.

Another type of drier frequently used in the beauty parlor is the cabinet type, where the Poodle is placed in a square cabinet through which hot air is electrically blown. The authors while retaining an open mind have still to be convinced that this type of drier is a humane contrivance, and that it does not cause panic in the Poodle or, at the very least, discomfort.

Scissors

In addition to the above equipment, a suitable type of scissors must be chosen. There is generally a large assortment from which to make a selection. The authors very much favor scissors forged in France, or, as a second choice, ones of German manufacture. However, this is a personal choice and does not mean that scissors forged in other countries are not equally efficient. French scissors usually are extremely delicate in balance and light to use, while German scissors are somewhat heavier in build, but the forging is good. Scissors made of stainless steel, open jointed, with a finger rest, and measuring seven inches, are probably the most suitable for the job, but those forged from blue steel will also give good performance. Point-end blades are preferable for trimming Poodles than round-end blades, and curved shanks are extremely useful. Thinning, or tapering, scissors should never be used on Poodles' coats.

A pair of small forceps, a dental scaler, and a small cross-cut file will also be needed to complete the list.

For the Bath

But there are still a few items needed for the job of bathing and shampooing. A number of drying towels will be needed, a small bowl or measure for mixing the shampoo, a rubber mat for the bottom of the bath or sink, and a rubber spray unit with sprinkler head, for fixing to the faucet. A cork or foam mat, on which to sit the Poodle on the table while being dried, is an asset.

Daily Grooming

So having decided the items of equipment we shall need, or perhaps what is more important – those which we can afford – we can think about the actual grooming and shampooing.

Grooming is perhaps the most important part of the Poodle's toilet. The Poodle's coat is quite unique, for he does not shed. This is a great advantage, for it obviates the nuisance of hairs on chairs, carpets and clothing. It also means that anyone suffering from Asthma may safely own a Poodle. However, there is a negative side to it because, of course, the dead hair must go somewhere, and in the Poodle, the old hair at certain times of the year forms small "tags" which, if neglected, work into tangles and then into felty mats. So, if his coat is to remain in tiptop shape it is absolutely essential that the Poodle be *groomed down to the skin* regularly – at least three days a week. When this actual coat-changing takes place (and it is quite easy to discover, for the small tags will be seen in the coat, and come out with the comb) grooming must be carried out *daily without fail* for a matter of a week or ten days. If these tags are not removed, mats will form overnight, and if neglected, the entire coat will have to be cut down to the skin. So take immediate action.

The Poodle should be taught from the age of eight weeks or so that he must lie on his side for most of the grooming time. He will soon accept this if you are really firm to begin with, and insist that he lie still every time he attempts to wriggle. He should lie first on the right side and then on the left. The hair, having been parted down the middle of his back, must be brushed and then combed in layers from neck to tail. Brush firmly for a minute or two, and then take the coarse comb right down to the skin along the side of the body and down the fore and hind leg. Then the Poodle should be turned over, and the same procedure carried out on the other side.

When both sides are completed, the Poodle must be praised, and then sat up facing you while you groom down his chest and under his arms (which he will hate!). Then turn him so that he stands with his rear facing you, to enable you to brush and comb around his rump and down his hind legs, and his tail. Finally, comb his topknot, and then praise and reward him for behaving well.

The authors cannot stress too strongly the importance of this daily grooming. A Poodle who is a mass of tangles and mats is a disgrace, and such a coat condition is extremely unhygienic for it undoubtedly invites the presence of fleas and other pests. Never attempt to bathe a Poodle unless he has been well groomed right down to the skin just beforehand, because if there *are* any tangles, they will felt up when water and a cleansing agent are employed. They are then virtually impossible to remove except by scissoring which will spoil the coat.

The danger time for coat-changing is when the Poodle is from 11 to 12 months old, and it lasts from one to two weeks. Afterwards, early spring, and sometimes fall, can be danger times. As the Poodle grows older, the coat is far less inclined to tangle, and indeed, after the age of five, grooming can take place at much longer intervals, possibly only once a week, and no tangling will be experienced.

Bathing

It does not seem to matter how often a Poodle is bathed; many show dogs are shampooed once or even twice a week, but possibly the ideal period is once every two weeks. Just before the Poodle is to be put into the bath, he must be allowed plenty of opportunity to relieve himself; during this time the bathing apparatus can be assembled.

Two clean towels will be required, a small piece of cotton, the shampoo put ready in a measure or bowl, the spray attached, and the rubber mat placed in the bath or sink. The drier should be in place, and a clean brush and comb handy. After the Poodle has been groomed carefully, both ears should be firmly plugged with a little cotton, for if water gets into the ear channel it may cause a bout of canker. If his eyes are sensitive to shampoo, a smear of petroleum jelly should be put on the lids and gently massaged over the eyeballs.

The Poodle should then be placed in the bath, and wetted all over, with the exception of his face and head, with warm water. The temperature should be around 100° to 120°. A good test is to feel the water with your elbow, and if it is just comfortable it will be right. After wetting him all over, apply the shampoo to his back and body, massaging well and working up a strong lather. Then wash front and hind legs in the same way, not forgetting his tail and between his toes. Finally, wet his face and head, and thoroughly wash these, taking care to keep the shampoo out of his eyes. Next, spray off the shampoo, and thoroughly rinse the coat for several minutes.

If a spray is not available, sponging with several changes of clean water must be employed. Squeeze the water from as much of the coat as possible, and then let Poodle Shake thoroughly. (It is quite easy to teach him the word "shake" and very useful). Then rub him all over with a warm towel, particularly on his back and under his belly; finally squeeze his fore and hind legs in the towel to remove as much moisture as possible.

Take a second warm towel and wrap him up in this tightly, and make him lie on the table. With a drier, first dry his ears and top-knot, brushing out the hair, and then combing it while the hot air from the dryer is still directed at his ears and head. As he has been wrapped in a towel, his coat will have been drying quite well; the towel should now be removed and the rest of the Poodle dried either lying down or standing, whichever suits you best. While continuing to dry him, brush the coat until it is three quarters dry, and then comb him until each hair is separated and quite dry. Don't forget to remove the ear plugs. Allow the Poodle a short time indoors in the warmth to "cool off" before letting him out.

Shampoo

The choice of shampoo is important; to imagine that any shampoo is good enough for a dog is indeed a bad policy. One of the primary causes of a dowdy coat is the indiscriminate use of harsh shampoos containing harmful detergents. Such shampoos can often produce skin rashes. As a result, the dog, in irritation, scratches the coat and breaks the hair. On the other hand, many owners use only the best shampoos intended for human hair, but again, this type of shampoo may not be suitable. It may contain agents to promote a soft and silky hair texture which is undesirable in the Poodle.

The ideal shampoo is one which contains a certain amount of oil with no harsh detergents. When rinsing off certain shampoos, it will be noticed that a thick lime scum floats on the water; such a shampoo is to be avoided. Shampoos containing a large percentage of soap are also harmful, for when the Poodle is dry the soap will be evident in the coat like scurf, or dandruff. So look for a shampoo which is oily, soapless and especially prepared for the Poodle coat.

A rinse containing pure lemon juice, or else a teaspoonful of vinegar, will usually clear the coat of any lime deposit, or soapiness, and promote a fine gloss. An application of lanolin cream before the final rinse will also improve the coat condition.

There are many shampoos prepared especially for Poodles – some containing beer, coconut oil, and egg, as well as other substances. There are also a variety of shampoos prepared for special colors. In each case these preparations enhance a particular shade and bring out the highlights of the coat. In addition, deodorizing sprays incorporating eau de cologne and lavender water, and others which impart a splendid luster to the coat, are available. In fact, no other breed of dog probably has so many special toilet aids as does the Poodle.

Nail Care

The care of the feet, ears and teeth is an important part of the Poodle's toilet. Undoubtedly the best time to trim the nails is immediately after a bath when the nails are soft and are not likely to split or break. It is not difficult, although many Poodles hate having it done. Of course, it is much easier to cut a light nail than it is to cut a black or dark nail, because, when unpigmented, the pink quick can easily be seen. When the nails are black, a novice should nip off only the tip and then file down the rest of the nail to the proper length as without experience there really is no way of knowing exactly where the quick begins.

When cutting the nail, grasp the Poodle's foot in your left hand and press the nail and pad between your thumb and first finger,

When cleaning your dog's ear, never poke too deeply with forceps or cotton swabs. A safe rule to follow: never poke deeper than you can see.

and use the nail clippers sharply and decisively with your right hand. Pressing the nail and pad ensures a steady grasp, and also serves to deaden the nerve in the nail while you are clipping.

If by any chance you do cut too close to the quick and cause bleeding, it can be stopped immediately by dipping the nail into crystals of permanganate of potash, so always keep some handy. Nails may be filed to add the finishing touch; a small crosscut file should be used. Again press the nail and pad with your left hand, and use the file in an upward direction. At first you will find that you are not getting the nails very short; but if you file them regularly once or twice a week, the quicks will recede, and the Poodle will soon acquire a lovely foot, well muscled up with neat short nails.

Ear Care

Ears need a certain amount of attention. Poodles, like other breeds, are prone from time to time to ear trouble. As has been mentioned, it is important to plug the ears before shampooing, because water seeping into the ear can cause a great deal of trouble. In any case, the ears should be dried out completely after bathing, by using cotton to remove even the slightest moisture. As a maintenance precaution, ears may be dusted with a canker prevention powder, or a dust of boracic powder, once a week. If ear trouble is present, it can usually be recognized either by a somewhat unpleasant odor, or by a squelching sound which can be heard while gently massaging the ear; it is unwise to poke too deeply about in the dog's ear with forceps or cotton swabs for these may cause damage to the inner ear. It is safer to seek veterinary advice.

Dental Care

Teeth normally need little attention. If the Poodle is given hard biscuit, and large beef bones, he will keep his teeth white and shining. However, tartar that forms on the enamel can be chipped off with dental scalers, either by yourself or the veterinarian, but such tartar is usually present only when the care of the teeth has been neglected, or in old Poodles. Teeth should be cleaned regularly with a baby tooth brush and a good quality tooth powder. Another excellent cleaning mixture is one part peroxide of hydrogen and one part fresh cold milk. A piece of cotton soaked in this solution and rubbed briskly on the teeth will help to keep them white and shining, and the peroxide will lessen any tendency to gum shrinkage, and the consequent falling out of teeth.

Parasites

This appears to be a good place to deal with the problem of coat parasites. These unpleasant pests – fleas, lice, ticks and harvest mites – can all cause havoc with the show coat. The flea also acts as host to the tapeworm, and brings an added danger. Fleas are adept at running through the coat at great speed when disturbed, and they are also long distance hoppers. The male flea is very small indeed, and black in color, while the female is a little larger, and brown. The most effective flea control is by using the "90 Day"^{TM}dog collar Worn around the dog's neck, this collar eliminates fleas anywhere on the body for three full months. It also helps in the control of ticks.

Lice are even more unpleasant and do more damage. They are grey in color, and move very very slowly. They nest in numbers, usually on the ear leathers, in the topknot, around the tail, on the sides of the belly and down the legs. They burrow into the skin and scythe down the hair, leaving bare or short patches in the coat. If a dog has short fringes on his leathers, a topknot which will not grow profuse, and furrows on both shoulders, giving his mane the appearance of a ballet dancer's tutu, suspect the presence of lice.

The treatment is a bath in some strong wash specifically prepared to destroy these pests, and yet not harm the coat. Give a second bath in ten days time; this will destroy all the lice from eggs unhatched at the time of the first bath. A third bath at three weeks should then

Teeth normally need little attention other than regular cleaning which the owner can usually do himself.

completely rid the Poodle of both fleas and lice. All bedding must be burnt; rugs and blankets, brushes and combs should be washed in a strong disinfectant.

Ticks are another problem; they are usually picked up from foliage or grass where other animals have passed. They can also be brought into the home on plants. The tick has tiny legs, and a protruding mouth which bores into the flesh of the dog. It then begins to suck blood, and grows a body or "container" for the eggs, which is green or purple-colored, distinctly resembling a pea in size. It is not advisable to try to pick or pull the tick from the Poodle's skin. If this is done, the pea like body usually bursts, leaving the head buried in the skin, and an unpleasant abscess forms. The tick should either be anesthetized with chloroform, or soaked in alcohol, or, with a steady hand, a lighted cigarette may be held against the tick's body. The tick will then release its hold on the skin and can be picked off; it should then be burned immediately.

Harvest mites make their appearance around harvest time. They are picked up by the dog while walking in fields where grain has been harvested; they are usually found in the wrist and ankle ruffles or in the ear fringes. Harvest mites are minute, bright orange in color, and resemble grains of cayenne pepper. They cause appalling irritation, but shampooing in a Gammexane solution will get rid of them.

To sum up, groom your Poodle regularly right down to the skin, using the correct equipment. Find a suitable shampoo and shampoo regularly, and don't forget to comb out the hair as you dry it. Some shampoos contain insecticides and thus disinfect as they clean. Inspect nails, ears and teeth every week, taking the necessary steps to keep them clean and free from trouble. Your Poodle will then be healthy, hygienic and happy.

154

This is American Champion Gimmick De Gillen. An outstanding silver Toy, Gimmick is shown at ten months of age in a puppy clip, and at two years of age in the English Saddle clip after having completed his championship. Gimmick is owned by Michael Gillen.

XII   Basic Clipping

The Poodle coat needs considerable care. And this care can cost a lot of money. Grooming parlors will undertake the regular maintenance of your Poodle's coat including clipping it into whatever style you fancy. But such treatment can quite easily be carried out at home, and in the last chapter all the equipment needed was fully discussed.

Some people can learn the art of clipping in a surprisingly short while; obviously they have a natural aptitude. Others find it more difficult to master. But if you follow our directions carefully, you should soon be able to clip your own Poodle so that he can compete with the best.

Clipping the Puppy

Not all Poodles take kindly to the clippers; others seem to have no fear whatsoever. Success probably lies in first clipping the puppy when he's as young as possible – in fact, six weeks old is not too young. If this is done regularly, the Poodle will regard clipping and trimming and all that goes with it as a normal course of events. But if he is not introduced to the clipping procedure until older, he is likely to object very strongly indeed.

SALLY ANNE THOMPSON

The puppy clip is accepted by the American Kennel Club for the show ring.

Initially, it is a great help to switch on the clippers and hold them in view of the puppy for several minutes, and let him become accustomed to the noise. Then very gently lay the clippers on part of his body, drawing them backwards, but do not attempt to cut the hair. This will get him used to the feel of vibration on his body.

Be very sure that the table you are using is completely steady, and that it has a nonskid surface. Nothing terrifies a dog more than the feeling that he may be going to fall. Always test the heat of the blades during clipping, since sometimes they become extremely hot and can cause unpleasant burns. Also, keep the blades of both your clippers and your scissors really sharp and properly ground. Blunt blades are inclined to nick the skin and spoil the finish of the coat, while dull scissors pull the hair as they cut, causing the Poodle to become fidgity and testy.

A.—Detail of holding dog while scissoring pompon.
B.—Preferred way to hold scissor.
C.—Recommended way to hold clipper.

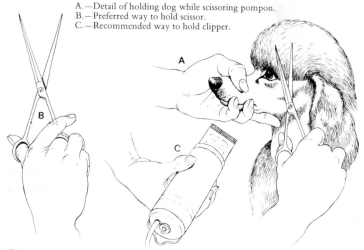

156

Be as kind and gentle as possible, but be firm. Your Poodle must be made to realize that you are not going to put up with a lot of nonsense! But anyone who handles a Poodle roughly, or who loses his temper when matters become a little exasperating, will get absolutely nowhere. The Poodle himself will become upset and lose his head, and this will lead to complete non-cooperation. On the other hand, you must not give up if the Poodle becomes difficult because if he feels he has got the upper hand and forced you to give up the struggle, he will never cooperate with you again. So, with kindness and gentleness allied to firmness and perseverance, all will be well.

All Poodles are given the basic clip – the clipping of the face, the feet and the tail. These three parts of the anatomy are clipped no matter what style is preferred with a few variations in the wearing of moustaches and whiskers. The puppy has his feet, face and tail clipped from the age of six to eight weeks throughout his life, and these areas will need to be clipped regularly every eight or nine weeks.

Presuming that you are right-handed, you should hold your dog as illustrated in the diagram, using your left hand, and taking up the clippers in your right hand. Use the clippers on the hair in the opposite way to which it grows, (the arrows indicate the direction) and aim at a slow steady stroke rather than short sharp jerks. You will find that you have a better surface for clipping if you pull the skin slightly downwards with your left hand, working your clippers upwards with the right. Lay the clippers flat on the skin, and tilt just slightly to take up the hair.

Clipping the Face

Now look at the next diagram and you will see that special lines must be followed, and you should aim first at clipping a perfectly straight line from the ear hole under the ear flap (point B) to the corner of the eye marked A. Then clip the cheek, and take a rounded line from point C 3 (under the chin on neck) up to the ear hole at point B. The same procedure should be followed on the other side of the face.

Next clip along the top of the muzzle from point D by the eyes to the nose at point E, and also clip in the same way along the sides of the muzzle. Take great care at point F which is the corner of the

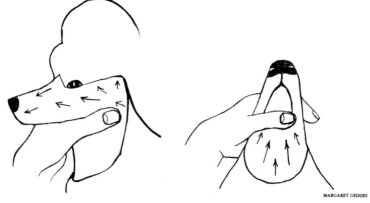

The position of hands, and direction of cut, while clipping the Poodle's face.

lips, as it is possible to snag the skin here. Finally, clip from the bottom of the neck, point C, taking off all the hair under the chin and lower jaw, up to the mouth (unless a moustache is required).

The line at the base of the neck should be taken from point C which is approximately two inches below the "Adam's apple" (the soft protruberance in the center of the throat), up to point G, the center of the lower lip.

The hair must be clipped neatly from below the eyes, and it will help if the skin is pulled down with your left thumb. Never under any circumstances must the hair be clipped from *above* the eyes, for this would give the Poodle an oddly startled expression; in any case it is incorrect. However, an inverted ∧ may be clipped from the inner corner of each eye, to a point about one inch upwards, as shown in diagram. This must be a narrow ∧ and it must give the impression of lengthening the head; it will also help to keep the hair out of the Poodle's eyes. Finally, carefully clip over the face to tidy up any small areas that may have been missed.

The only variations in these lines and measurements will be when it is desired to leave a moustache or whiskers on the face; for instance, in some types of Dutch or Lamb Trim.

If you are using electric clippers, either a 10 mm or a 15 mm blade would be suitable. You can, of course, use scissors, but obviously you will not get such a smart finish. While a 30 mm blade can be used, it will give a *very* close finish that should be attempted only by the expert.

Clipping the Feet

Most Poodles do not like to have their front feet clipped, although they behave better when the hind feet are clipped. Again clip the hair opposite to the way it grows, clip up from the nails, over the arched toes, to the ankle, stopping just below the ankle joint; this is approximately 1½ to 2 inches up from the floor. All the hair must be clipped from between the toes, and this is the difficult part. Pushing your second and third fingers into the pad underneath the foot will cause the dog to spread his toes, (see diagram) and if a small toe-blade on the electric clipper is used, you will find that the hair can be neatly removed. This can be accomplished equally well by the use of scissors.

It is also necessary to clip the hair from in between the pads, for if this is left, it is inclined to become caked with mud. Mud will spread the pads, and detract from the line of a slim, well muscled foot. When the foot has been neatly clipped, the hair on the leg may fall untidily over it, so this, too, must be neatly trimmed around with scissors just below the ankle joint. The Poodle is crafty, and since he does not like having his feet clipped he will try various subterfuges to keep you from it, often laying his chin on the foot, or dangling his ear fringes where your are about to clip. A control frame which is illustrated will help, or a stocking cap (described in the section on Nursing) may be put on during the operation. The same procedure is followed for the back feet, and here the clipping line should be taken to just below the hock joint.

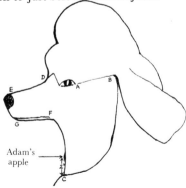

MARGARET GEDDES

Lines to be followed when clipping the face of the Poodle.

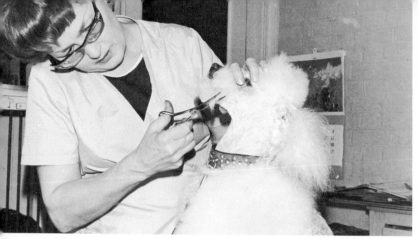

Fashioning a moustache and small beard for the Dutch clip.

Clipping the Tail

Practically all styles call for a "pom" on the end of the tail, but be careful when clipping this part of the Poodle's anatomy as it is exceedingly sensitive; he can suffer quite considerably from a "tickly tail" after a clipping session. It is advisable to work with a fairly coarse blade such as a 10 mm, or else to use scissors. The tail should be clipped from the root up towards the tip for approximately 1½ inches, leaving a good "pom" of about the same depth of 1½ inches. This refers to a tail of normal length. However, not all tails have been docked to a normal length – some are **very short** and some are over long, but you should be able to correct **the appearance** to a certain extent by judicial trimming and shaping (see Diagram).

If the tail is too short, then the clipped area must extend almost to the end of the tail, and in this case a long and profuse "pom" must be grown and carefully trimmed (see point D). But if the tail is over long, the same distance of 1½ inches should be clipped. It will be found that there is still about three inches covered by "pom," and therefore the long hair of the "pom" must be cut as close to the end of the tail stump as possible (see point C). The normal stump of tail on a Miniature Poodle should measure three inches, and the "pom" should extend beyond this for another 1 to 1½ inches. Tail poms take quite a time to mature profusely; it therefore pays to leave as much hair on the end of the stump as possible in a young Poodle.

This is the way the toes should be spread when clipping the feet.

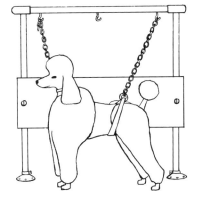

A clipping control frame which keeps the Poodle in the required position, but does not unduly restrict or frighten him.

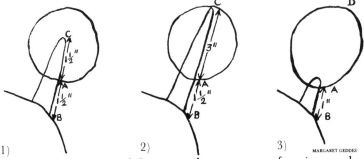

MARGARET GEDDES

Careful tail clipping can help correct the appearance of an improperly docked tail. 1) Correct length of tail. 2) Too-long tail. 3) Too-short tail.

Skin Irritation

Examine the clipped parts of the Poodle's skin very carefully to see that there are no scraped places or small nicks. In any case, it would be advisable to wipe all clipped parts with a soothing baby lotion. If a clipper rash should appear afterwards, the skin may be dabbed with benzyl benzoate which is extremely soothing and will kill any infection that may be present. An excellent powder (for white or light colored Poodles) is one made up of ¾ talcum powder and ¼ zinc oxide. Bathing before clipping will do much to obviate skin irritation and sensitivity.

You should now, after a little practice, have mastered the basic clipping of your Poodle, and can graduate to the more advanced styles.

Clipping Styles for Puppies

The usual style for a puppy is the First Puppy Clip; this is the basic clipping of face, feet and tail, as already described, and then a tipping of the coat all over to remove untidy ends. This tipping of the coat is done with scissors, the coat being trimmed down to approximately two inches on back, neck, chest, but left a little fuller on fore and hind legs. A puppy may appear in the show ring in this clip until he is 12 months old; he then officially leaves his puppyhood. However, most exhibitors and many owners of pets like to put their Poodles into a more adult style before the age of one year, and this is officially permissible.

There are two variations of the First Puppy Clip: the Pajama Clip and the Second Puppy Clip. In the Pajama Clip, the Poodle receives the basic clip. The mane which covers the shoulders, ribs and chest is allowed to grow as long as possible, but hair on the hind legs and front legs is cut moderately short in preparation for the next clip which will either be the Second Puppy Clip or the adult Traditional Lion Clip (or English Saddle Clip).

The Second Puppy Clip is usually adopted for Poodles of nine months of age or so, and here again there is the basic clip of face, feet and tail, the mane left as long as possible, but the front legs are clipped short from the ankle to elbow, leaving an anklet or bracelet covering the ankle joint as in the Lion Clip or English Saddle Clip. The hair on the hind quarters from the last rib, over the haunches, and right down to just below the hocks, is cut to a length of about two inches.

Both these last two puppy styles are primarily for show dogs, and the traditional adult show clip follows. Puppies that are to be eventually put into any of the non-show styles, Dutch Clip, Lamb Clip, Cowboy Clip, and so forth, would graduate straight from the First Puppy Clip, missing out on the Pajama Clip and the Second Puppy Clip.

Most of the adult clips are a little more difficult than the Puppy Clips, but we will try to explain them step by step in the following chapters.

Champion de Russy Necromancer, shown winning in a continental clip. This dog was shown a *total* of 13 times in his entire life and has five Best of Varieties, one Group First and two Group Seconds. He is 25 inches of elegant Standard Poodle. Owned by de Russy Kennels Registered of California, and handled by Phyllis Greer before the English judge, Mr. Butcher.

XIII Clipping the Show Poodle

This and the next chapter dealing with the various clipping styles have been subdivided into show clips and companion clips. The division is very marked indeed for the two general styles of clipping could not be more different – in fact, they are the direct opposite

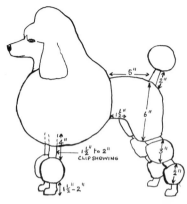

Measurements for clipping the Miniature Poodle into show style. All measurements in these drawings are based on the Miniature Poodle. The measurements can easily be adjusted up for a Standard or down for a Toy.

A superbly-coated black Miniature Poodle in the traditional Lion clip. Ear fringes have grown to a phenomenal length.

in every way. In show clipping, the hair on the legs is almost all shaved away, and the body hair (or mane is grown as long as possible, while in companion Poodle clipping the hair on the legs is often left to grow to an exaggerated length, and the hair on the body is clipped short or shaved.

It is often said that the style adopted for companion Poodles tends to cover up a multitude of sins in action and leg formation, while show clipping exposes leg formation at a glance. If the Poodle is to be exhibited he must conform to, and appear in one of the permitted Show clips, but if he has no aspirations for the Show ring he can be given whichever clip this owner pleases. This does not mean to say, of course, that a companion Poodle cannot wear the traditional show clip. Many owners of companion Poodles prefer the conventional or traditional styles and, indeed, are of the opinion that these styles enhance the dog's elegance and dignity.

But for the moment we are considering clipping styles for the show ring, and as we noted before for the adult Poodle these are three in number: the Traditional Lion Clip (which is favored almost exclusively in the English show ring), the English Saddle Clip (which, conversely, is used in the American show ring), and the Continental Clip which is used in both countries, and in many other European countries. There is not a tremendous difference between these three clips, but you should know exactly what these differences are.

In addition to the three styles for adults, there is also the Puppy Clip described in the previous chapter, and the Pajama Clip and Second Puppy Clip, but these two are not accepted by the Kennel Club in America for the show Poodle, although they are, in England.

To put a Poodle into show clip is not easy; to begin with, it will take quite a long time, possibly several hours. However, with considerable practice, the groomer will become very adept, and it then will be possible to shape a Poodle in under an hour.

It must be pointed out that the following measurements refer to an average sized Miniature Poodle. For a Toy Poodle, reduce the measurements, and for the Standard Poodle increase them proportionately.

The Traditional Lion Clip

The basic clipping of face, feet and tail was demonstrated in the last chapter. Again let us repeat that until you are expert in the use of clippers you should not use a blade finer than 15 mm, though the 30 mm blade is generally used by the expert to prepare the show Poodle.

Stage I

Have ready a well-balanced sharp pair of 7 inch scissors, a chromium plated brass comb, the clippers of your choice, a stocking cap, and a piece of material measuring about 18 inches long and 8 inches wide, with tapes about 8 inches long sewn on each corner. This is used as a sort of cummerbund and its use will be described directly.

You now have your Poodle standing on the table, and you should refer to the diagram. First of all, decide exactly where the hair should be cut to leave the mane. To do this, a parting should be made in the hair all around the body at point X, and this parting line should eventually tally with the last rib on the body. However, it is advisable to run the parting slightly more towards the tail end, as it is common to find that you have cut the mane just too far up

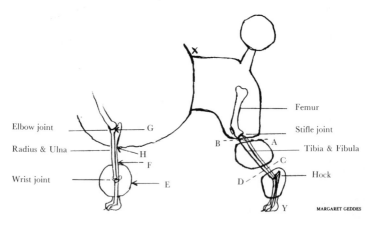

By following this lettered chart, you will be able to relate the pattern to the underlying bone formation.

X: The point in the middle of the back where the mane is to be begun.

A to B: narrow band cut just below the stifle joint.

C to D: A narrow band just below the hock. Notice that this slants at about 45 degrees.

E: Placement of wrist ruffle.

F: Point at which leg clipping begins above the ruffle.

G: The elbow joint where leg clipping ends.

H: The mane covers the elbow joint to a point two inches below.

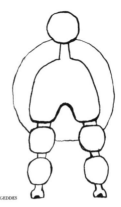

Inspect the Poodle from the rear to make sure that the hair is uniform all around.

the body. If you leave a little more mane than really necessary, it is easy to trim it off when finishing, but if the mane is too short, you cannot put the hair back!

When you have a really even parting around the Poodle's body, define this more completely by brushing from point X to the tail, and then use your cummerbund over the body part of the mane, tying the tapes around the parting line and around the neck. This will keep the mane safely out of the way and there is now no fear of your cutting it by mistake, or losing your marking. Then rough off the hair with the scissors from the parting line X, over the

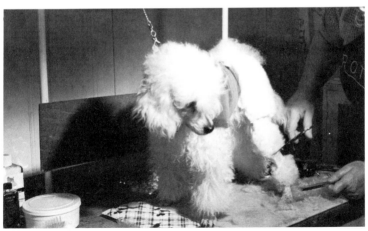

Show preparation. Shaping the ruffles on hind legs and showing use of a body band to keep the mane out of the way of damage.

The trials of show business! Here an apricot show dog is having his ear fringes rolled in material to protect the ends from splitting. This method keeps both the ear fringes and the topknot in perfect condition, and free from food particles which may stick to the hair. The rollers are taken off just before the Poodle enters the ring.

haunches and down over each hind leg, leaving the hair at 1½ inches graduating to 2 inches at the hocks at point Y.

Stage II

This next stage is difficult and needs practice, for now you are going to shape the ruffles around the stifle joints, and shape the anklets at the hock joints. The easiest method to work is by feeling the structure of the bones with your fingers. Cut a narrow band in the hair with the scissors from point A to B, and this must go around the leg; it should be just below the stifle joint (see diagram 28). With your fingers you can feel where the femur bone is joined to the fibula and tibia bones at the stifle joint. Cut a similar line on the other leg.

If you turn your Poodle with his tail towards you, you should be able to gauge whether the lines you have cut are straight and match each other (see diagram). Next, cut another band from C to D immediately above the hock joint. This line must slant slightly downwards from point C to D. Having satisfied yourself that each pair of bands is straight and evenly placed, and that the measurements of both stifle and hock ruffles are approximately those given in diagram 28, your next job is to clip the bands with the clippers to a depth of approximately ¾ inch. Beware here, because it is very easy to clip too wide a band.

Stage III

You are now ready to shape the hair on the loins and hips with scissors, to a length of about ¾ to one inch. This should be carefully done with the scissors flat against the hair, until the hair resembles plush or pile. The quick but lazy way to trim the lower back and loins is to use the 5 mm cutter head, clipping the way the hair grows, but this will not give as smart a finish as scissoring.

Next the stifle, or middle ruffle, must be neatly scissored, and here the hair may be left just slightly longer. Finally, trim the bottom or hock anklet, again leaving the hair just a little fuller. The measurements detailed in diagram 28 will help you to get the correct measurements on a normal sized Miniature Poodle.

It is well to give your Poodle the opportunity to stretch his legs at this point. And the cummerbund can now be removed.

Stage IV

To commence the front leg shaping, stand the Poodle facing you. You have already clipped the feet to approximately one inch below the wrist joint. Slip the stocking cap over the Poodle's head to keep his ears from interfering. The wrist ruffle should cover the wrist joint E, approximately one inch above and one inch below. Therefore, part the hair one inch above the wrist joint, point F. Hold the wrist in your left hand, up to the parting, and then with scissors rough off the long hair up to the elbow joint (under the mane) from F to G. Check that you have an even parting around the wrist at F, and then clip the hair neatly all around the leg up to the actual elbow joint. Repeat the process on the other leg.

Stage V

Now the wrist ruffles and ankle ruffles must be shaped, and a "snowball" effect achieved. To get this effect, three sub-stages must be followed (see diagram):

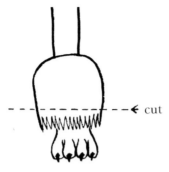

A. Combed down

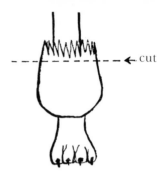

B. Combed up

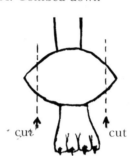

C. Combed to middle

D. Completed

How to shape the wristlets and anklets.

A. Comb the hair of the ruffle over the foot and neatly trim around the ends about 1½ inches from the ground.
B. Next, comb the hair upwards and trim the hair at the top.
C. Comb the hair upwards and downwards towards the middle of the ruffle, and then trim it off neatly around the sides. Finally, trim off any odd ends and pieces; you should now have produced a smart snowball effect as shown in the diagram.

Stage VI

Now we come to the final trimming of the mane, and this should be vigorously brushed back from the loins up to the head; neatly trim off any straggling ends, aiming at the effect of a well-rounded muff. You will probably find the hair straggling over the elbows and below the chest, and the correct and careful shaping of these parts will really add to the final smartness of your Poodle. Comb the

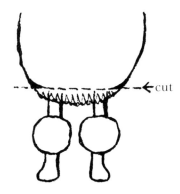

Where to trim the mane at the front of the chest for the final effect.

hair downwards at point H over the elbows, and neatly trim it so that about 1½ to 2 inches of the clipped part of the front leg is now showing. Turn the Poodle facing you and continue trimming across the lower part of the chest between the front legs, and around to the other elbow.

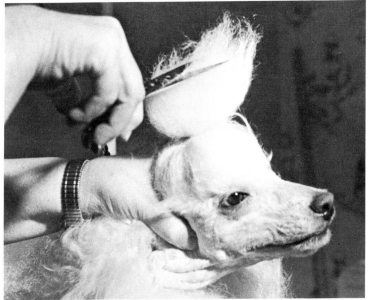

Shaping the top-knot after confining the hair with a rubber band.

The topknot is one of the important features of the Poodle head and must be protected when he is away from the ring. This American Champion's owner uses a piece of plastic which will remain in place until the dog is ready to be groomed for show.

Styles for clipping Poodles do not vary too much from country to country. This Poodle, photographed in Sweden, is in the English Saddle clip.

This Swedish Poodle does credit to the Continental clip. Only a Poodle with faultless hind action can afford to wear it. It is slightly different from the Continental clip we are accusomed to. Pompons on the haunches are optional. In 1965 Champion Pierre Boy was selected Dog of the Year in Sweden.

MARGARET GEDDES

Hair styling. A: Puppy style with bow or grip. B: Adult show clip with backward look, and C: With older forward look. D: Style usually adopted in Continental clip. E: Moustache in Continental clip.

Stage VII

Finally, only the topknot remains to be attended to, and the diagram will help you do that. Gather up the hair from both sides of the forehead and from the back of the head, and slip a small rubber band around it. The top ends will probably be a little uneven; to achieve a smart finish, gather the hair above the band with the closed fist of your left hand, and cut off about ½ inch of hair in a straight line above your hand. When released, the hair will fan out into a good plume.

There are two styles for wearing the topknot; you can either pull the band backwards, which takes the hair well back from the forehead, and gives the impression of elongating the head. This suggests a softer expression and is particularly suitable for females and young males. Otherwise, the forward style can be adopted: draw the hair forward from the back of the head towards the eyes, and then slip on the band. This creates an older and more sophisticated expression. These hair styles are usual in the English show ring, but in America the use of a slide or clip is more popular. This creates

173

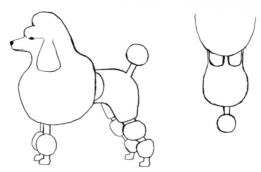

Details of the English Saddle Clip.

a swept back look, allowing the hair on the head and above the ears to billow out, giving a halo effect. It is most attractive. When removing the rubber band, it is advisable to cut it away. Bands are inexpensive and trying to pull one off means that some of the hair may be pulled out too.

Finally, it is time to do the pompon on the tail. The actual pom should be 3 to 4 inches in length; the closely clipped part near the rump, 2 inches. Take the hair of the pom in your left hand, and scissor straight across the top, taking off about ½ inch of hair, and then trim off any odd edges. Another method is to twist the hair of the pompon with finger and thumb and then scissor off ½ inch from the end. When released, the pom will untwist and fly out into a round ball. Methods for helping to shape a pom on a tail that has been docked either too short or too long, were discussed in the last chapter.

You now have only to brush your Poodle's mane upwards at the

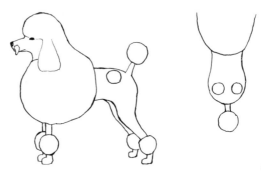

Details of the Continental clip, shown here with pompons. The pompons are optional.

sides, chest, and along the back, and trim off any taggy ends that spoil the outline; stand him up in the show position and you should have a dog of which you can be proud.

The English Saddle Clip

This is much the same as the traditional Lion Clip, with one small variation. This consists of clipping a crescent shaped patch between the haunches and the mane on either side of the body. The fullness on the hindquarters is known as the "pack". Between the mane and the pack make a long, crescent shaped indentation on each side of the body. The diagram illustrates the style. Everything else is exactly the same as the Lion Clip.

The Continental Clip

This is slightly different. It is a most attractive style, but only a Poodle with faultless hind action can afford to wear it. The hair is shaved closely from the end of the mane at the last rib, right over the haunches and down each leg, leaving a full anklet on the hind hock. Usually two circles of hair are left just by the hip joint; and these circles or rosettes should measure approximately 2½ to 3 inches in diameter. They should be separated on top by the width of the clipper blade. To get an even round, a cup or glass may be placed on the hair, and a line clipped round to give the shape and position of the rosettes, before the quarters are closely clipped. Each rosette should be combed from the center outwards, and the edges trimmed round, so that they are ball-like. Some owners favor more exaggerated decoration by shaping these patches into hearts and other patterns, but the round rosette is the most common; it carries out the line of the round mane and the tail pom and bracelets.

With the Continental Clip it is permissible for the Poodle to wear a *very* small moustache, just below the nose on the upper lips. Also in this style, the hair on the head is not shaped into a topknot or a pom, but is kept shorter and swept back. Sometimes a clip or barrette is used. The mane is a little shorter and less full than in the other styles. It is a clip admirably suited to the lean and elegant Poodle with long legs, but is not in the least suitable for the Poodle who is, perhaps, a little more than well covered, and a shade short on the leg.

Now, isn't he a lamb?

XIV Clipping the Companion Poodle

The styles evolved for the companion Poodle are many and various – perhaps more varied in the United States than in the United Kingdom. However, by far the two most popular ones are the Lamb or Curly Clip and the Royal Dutch Clip – the first seen more in England, the second more in America.

As companion Poodles do not always have the "perfect" points of the show Poodle, one style may suit one Poodle, while another style will bring out the best in a different dog.

Again it must be remembered that the measurements given refer to a normal sized Miniature Poodle, and are to be increased or decreased according to the size of your dog.

The Lamb Clip

This clip is also known as the Curly Clip, the Country, or the Astrachan Clip. The Poodle is first given the basic clip of face, feet and tail, but since a moustache *may* be desired, the muzzle must not be clipped clean until this point has been decided.

There is not a great deal to describe in this clip – in fact, the three words "cut it short' would suffice! But perhaps there is a little more to it than that. As when clipping all Poodles, yours must first be shampooed, and the hair carefully combed out while being dried. It is essential that no tangles or mats remain. Then, with scissors, shorten the coat all over the body (with the exception of the head and tail pom) to a length of ¾ inch or less. To do this, stand the Poodle with his stern towards you, and cut evenly up the back of the hind legs, over the haunches, around and over the ribs, around the neck and up to where the topknot begins at the base of the skull.

The belly and chest are also scissored very close. But the hair on the fore and hind legs should be fashioned rather more fully to a length of possibly one to 1½ inches. This fullness should start over the buttocks on the hind quarters, and over the shoulders on the fore quarters. To achieve a satisfactory rounded finish on the legs, hold the hind foot in the left hand and extend the leg out backwards. This will facilitate the even scissoring of the coat. Do the same with the fore leg, but extend it out towards the front with the Poodle facing you.

If you can learn to scissor the hair over the comb, you will obtain a much better finish, and, with practice, the coat can be made to resemble a really thick plush, but this technique does need practice. The routine is to push the comb into the hair *against* the way it grows, then lift the comb a fraction to give a little more length to the hair which you wish to leave on, and then the hair appearing *above* the comb is scissored off. When you become expert in this method you will be able to cut the coat perfectly evenly to any length from about ⅛ inch to 3 inches. This way cutting has the added advantage of safeguarding the Poodle's skin.

The tail bears the usual pom on the end, though some prefer to clip the tail short all over.

The topknot is cut with an even round. To do this, starting at the center of the skull comb the hair outwards all around, giving it a

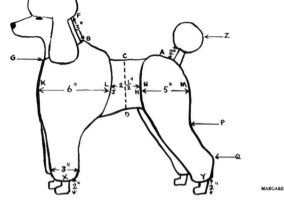

Measurements for the Dutch clip. These are scaled for the Miniature Poodle.

flat appearance. Then trim the ends which are in a flat circle all around the head. Comb the hair up into its normal position and you should have a well-rounded topknot. If a shorter topknot is required, the hair can be reduced by shaping all over. The ears may either be left fully fringed or they may have the hair scissored or clipped from the leathers, leaving a small fringe only on the ends.

Undoubtedly, better results are obtained with the expert use of scissors, but if time is important, the entire style may be achieved with the 5 mm clipper head, except for the head and tail which must be scissored.

A severe variation of this style, one favored by sportsmen and country folk who train the Poodle to the gun, is to clip the Poodle entirely with 5 mm or 7 mm blades, including feet, face, tail and ears.

The Royal Dutch Clip

So called because the heavy shoulder and haunch pads, fore and aft, resemble the voluminous trousers of the Dutch peasant; where the word "Royal" comes from, history does not relate! When doing this clip it is important that the measurements and marking lines be kept even. This often presents a difficulty if the Poodle is inclined to be fidgety. The usual face, feet and tail basic clipping is carried out, but again the muzzle should not be clipped if a moustache is desired.

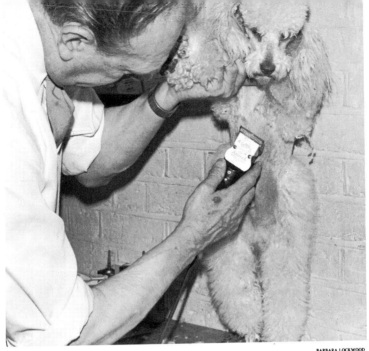

Dutch clip. Clipping the belly while holding the Poodle standing on his hind legs. This is the best way of controlling him.

Stage I

With the 10 mm blade used *against* the way the hair grows, or with the 15 mm blade in the opposite direction, clip a line (see diagram) from the root of the tail at A straight up to the base of the skull at B, strictly following the backbone. Use the clippers with a slow and even movement; do not jerk. Next, clip a similar band around the body, over the rib cage, and under the belly (C to D) taking as the approximate measurement for this where the last two ribs are situated. You will now have clipped a cross on the Poodle's back.

Stage II

Fasten a narrow collar *very loosely* around the Poodle's neck, letting the collar hang like a necklace. Refer to the diagram and clip the hair from the line of the collar at point B up to the base of the skull, and around to the basic clip line at the throat point G following the line of the collar or necklace.

179

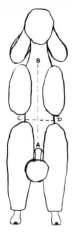

View from above showing the outline of the body clipping for the Dutch clip.

MARGARET GEDDES

Stage III

You will now see the idea of the outline of the high shoulder and haunch pads which typify this style. With the clippers, round off the pads as shown in both diagrams. The width of the forelegs should be approximately 6 inches from L to K, tapering to 3 inches at X, while the hind legs should measure 5 inches from M to N, and taper to 3 inches at Y. The long hair on the legs must be left rather full over the shoulders and haunches, possibly 2 to 2½ inches long, tapering down slightly at wrists and shoulders. To accentuate the natural angulation of the hind legs, the hair should be trimmed in slightly at point P and out again at the hock at point Q, taking down to ankle at Y. The hair on the legs will be rather long and shaggy, so it must be shortened to the length mentioned above. To do this, stand the Poodle with his rear towards you, and with your left hand stretch his leg out backwards. It will be much easier to scissor off the hair evenly. Do the same with the fore legs, but stand or sit the Poodle facing you, and extend the leg forward. The hair on all four legs should now be even, bushy and springy, and wherever the hair is shorter there should be an impression of plush or thick pile. Where the pads meet the shortly clipped hair of the body, the hair should be bevelled or barrelled as a finish.

Stage IV

The shaping of the topknot now needs attention. (See diagram). There is either the round topknot where the hair is bevelled off all round, to an even length of approximately one inch, or a much

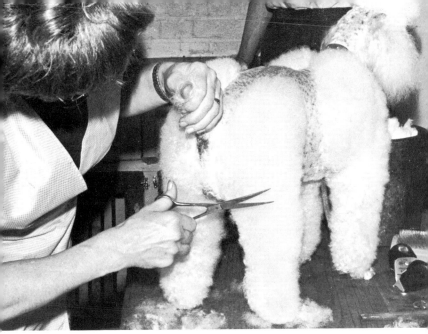

Dutch clip. Scissoring the back legs while keeping control of the Poodle by holding the tail.

fuller topknot rounded off to an approximately 3 inch length of hair. The hair at the base of the skull at the neck can be either rounded, or shaped into a "V".

To achieve a really smart topknot is difficult, but the illustration will help to show how. First, make a parting in the middle of the topknot on the top of the head, and then comb the hair downwards around the head from the central spot. Scissor the hair all around the head to a length of approximately 3 inches. Comb the hair upwards and backwards. It should now have become a well-rounded "pom," but may need trimming where there are uneven ends.

The tail in the Dutch Clip should be full and completely round (see point Z). The hair may either be combed out sideways all around and then trimmed with scissors; or the hair on the end of the tail may be twisted to an end, and this end scissored off. The tail when released should then fly out into a pom. It is immaterial whether a moustache is worn or not. Very often the males have them, while the females are cleanshaven, but it is really a matter of personal choice.

181

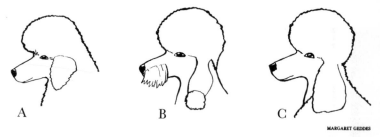

Various hair styles. A: Puppy head in either show or companion clip. B: Companion clip style with moustache and tassels on the end of the shaven ear. C: Clean-shaven style and topknot suitable for the companion Poodle.

Various Styles

It seems that the Poodle has come in for more than his fair share of curious and even fantastic clipping styles. Some admittedly suit his somewhat clown like nature, but others are not "him" at all. Some owners like to clip their Poodles to resemble other breeds, and so one sees the Retriever Clip, the Terrier Clip, and the Water Spaniel Clip. In each of these, the poor Poodle is fashioned to resemble another breed. It seems unfair that because of a whim he must lose his identity, and surely he must wonder why his owner does not possess that breed instead!

Of the clips which are not seen too often perhaps the Clown Clip, the Hillbilly Clip, the Sailor Boy Clip and the Cowboy Clip are the most attractive.

The Clown Clip

This is based on the Continental Clip up to a point, for here the face and feet, and the entire body are clipped down to the skin, leaving the topknot on the head, the pom on the tail, and wrist and ankle ruffles on fore and hind legs. A moustache may be worn, but if so, it should be a small one, and only on the top lips; not on the chin.

The Hillbilly Clip

This eccentric clip is quite attractive. Here the front legs and feet are closely clipped to the elbow, the hind legs and feet to a compar-

This attractive style was developed in Berlin, Germany, where it is called the Caracul or Modern cut and is acceptable for show there.

ative line on the stifle. The tail is clipped, no pom is worn, and the ear leathers are closely shaven. Encircling the shoulders from lower neck to mid-ribs, a shawl of hair about 2 to 3 inches long is left, and two large pads of hair the same length left on either buttock. The topknot is rounded and moderately short, and whiskers cover the entire face, over the muzzle to about one inch below the eyes. The neck is shaved down to where the shoulder shawl commences.

The Sailor Boy Clip

This jolly, rakish clip is not unlike the Dutch Clip. Face, feet and tail are clipped. The topknot is rounded and a pom is left on the tail. A moustache is generally worn, and the ears close shaven. However, on the fore and hind legs the hair is left moderately long, and shaped at wrists and ankles to bellow out, giving the impression of bell bottom trousers.

The Cowboy Clip

Seen quite often in England as well as America, this greatly resembles the Dutch Clip. A closely clipped body, ears and feet, with a rounded topknot and a pom on the tail. But the hair on fore and hind quarters is left at an exaggerated length to give the impression of cowboy trousers. The whiskers are left on to resemble a hillbilly beard, covering the whole of the muzzle, cheek and chin; only the area for an inch below the eye is shaved.

The Baby Doll Clip

A very feminine clip indeed! And surely only to be worn by bitches. This clip is a mixture of English Saddle Clip and Dutch Clip. The face, feet, tail and body are closely clipped, but a rounded topknot and tail pom are worn. Around each shoulder is a large pack of hair, rather resembling a fur stole, reaching to the elbow. The legs are shaven, but a ruffle covers the wrist. There is also a pack of long hair on each buttock falling to the stifle. Then a clipped band of about 2 inches in depth, and a ruffle to cover the ankle. The ears are clipped closely and to within an inch of the end of the leather, and a thick tuft of hair is left dangling on the end.

There is undoubtedly a large selection of clipping styles from which to choose, but surely one's aim should always be to enhance the Poodle's beauty and elegance. To do this, it will be difficult to find a clip more admirable than the Traditional Lion Clip or English Saddle Clip for the show dog, or the Dutch Clip or Lamb Clip for the delightful companion Poodle.

The monkey clip.

The cowboy clip.

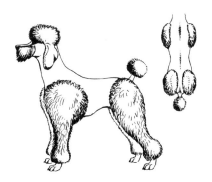

The sailorboy clip.

The hillbilly clip.

The clown cut.

185

Temperament is inherited as are physical characteristics. If you want calm, good-natured puppies then breed from parents with the desired temperament. It is easier to ruin a good dog with improper handling than it is to teach a nervous dog to be calm.

XV Breeding your Poodle

Dominant and Recessive Genes

Did you ever wonder why two black dogs, when mated, produce black puppies, and two white dogs produce white puppies? Occasionally, however, two black dogs are mated, and some of the puppies are white while others are black. Does all this happen by chance, or is there a definite pattern behind these apparently random happenings?

Years ago, a monk named Gregor Mendel studied this problem, using garden peas for his experiment. He found that characteristics are inherited according to certain fixed patterns and that taken on the average over large numbers, these patterns are rigid and relatively unswerving. These are known as the laws of inherited factors and the study devoted to them is called genetics.

To go into the science of genetics is outside the scope of a book of this type. However, if the reader will bear in mind that what follows is an oversimplification, we will try to outline some of the basic factors.

When a male and female mate, this is known as bi-sexual reproduction. The male reproductive particle, known as the sperm, joins the female reproductive particle which is called the egg or ovum. Every living creature has a fixed number of chromosomes in each cell, except for the sex cells. These contain half the requisite number. However, when the two sex cells join together to form the new unit, the combined total equals the proper number for the species. Chromosomes, under an electron microscope, resemble twisted threads with beads strung along them at intervals. These beads are known as genes, and they are concentrated "blueprints" which direct the development of the organism. There is a gene for every characteristic which the new life will contain. Half the blueprint comes from the mother, and half from the father.

Now, obviously, if a dog receives a factor of black from one parent and white from the other, it can't be both colors, nor will they blend into grey. One factor will dominate and determine the external characteristic. That is the characteristic we see. The other will not be lost but will be carried within the germ cells; it is known as a recessive. This recessive gene can be inherited through a number of generations, remaining concealed until at some future mating, it meets with its counterpart, another recessive, occupying the same position in the chromosome. The union of these two now appears and so we can understand why two black dogs suddenly produce a white puppy. Somewhere in the ancestry of each of the black dogs there was a white progenitor. Because white is recessive to black, this characteristic remained hidden until, more or less at random, the two white half-genes paired.

When the question of breeding puppies is being considered, it is most important that color inheritance is understood, and the pedigrees of both sire and dam be carefully studied to obviate as far as possible the breeding of hybrids, which in turn will breed mis-marks. These observations do not apply only the color, but equally as well to temperament, soundness, coat quality and many other attributes.

It is safe to say that if a desirable good point (such as a magnificent coat) is present in both parents, it will then also appear in at least a percentage of the offspring. Equally true, if a dog and a bitch with savage dispositions are mated, this fault, too, will be continued and some of the puppies will probably inherit appalling temperaments. So it is that an attribute, and, unfortunately, also a fault, can become well and truly stamped into a strain.

Linebreeding

A "strain" is a family or tribe of dogs all descended from each other, or related in some way, and puppies bred from such a strain are considered to be "linebred".

A dog brought in from another strain, and so not a true relation is referred to as an "outcross". Occasional outcrosses are brought into a strain to strengthen it in some specific point, but this may not always be wholly satisfactory, for while bringing in the required attribute, the outcross may also bring in characteristics which are definitely *not* desirable. Quite often two separate lines are bred within a strain, and dogs from each line are judiciously bred together, obviating the need for an outcross.

Inbreeding

This means breeding very close relations together, like father to daughter, mother to son, brother to sister. It is a dangerous policy unless heredity is completely understood, and is certainly not a practice to be indulged in by the amateur. It can only be carried out in the case of two well-nigh perfect specimens, since every characteristic will be fixed – good and bad.

A linebred relationship which often brings considerable success, is the mating of grandsire to granddaughter, or grandson to granddam, or uncle to niece, nephew to aunt, and half siblings (that is, dogs with the same fathers and different mothers, or alternatively the same mothers and different fathers), but the operative word must be *quality* on both sides if it is to be successful. The choice of the right stud for your bitch is an important matter that requires a lot of thought.

Inheritance of Poodle Color

A discussion of genes and chromosomes may seem tedious to owners of one pet Poodle, but to the serious breeder the study of inherited characteristics, especially coat color, is of the utmost importance.

We need first to describe the colors of our breed. The Poodle breeder uses different terms for certain colors than those used by owners of other breeds of dogs. For example, "liver" to a hound breeder may be equivalent to the "brown" of the Poodle breeder.

Black is a base color. It comes as true black, also as a mahogany black. But black is affected by other genes which modify it. A dilution gene can produce blue if it finds a partner like itself. The gene for blue is thus "recessive". This same gene can turn liver (brown) to pale brown.

But an inhibiting gene also affects black and produces liver colored coats and these dogs have liver colored noses and foot pads. Then there is the black which slowly changes to apricot as the puppy ages

What about white? We know there is the regular white, also a white spotted. In some rare breeds the white is dominant but not in Poodles because it is caused by a different gene, a recessive one. Poodles sometimes have a white coat with a cream tinge, and some silvers are so "bleached out" in appearance that they look white. Again, dogs of our breed are sometimes seen to be white but their history tells us they were born bleach, then changed to apricot and finally to white.

Apricot is a puzzling color. Some apricots are born rusty black. If they are born black or rusty black they usually carry gray or black hairs on the ears when mature. To make sure that a white is not an apricot, a lock of hair should be held against white paper. If you detect an ivory tint, you know that it is an apricot. Certain creams which some Poodle breeders call ivory, and others call cream white can be born cream colored while other creams are born black.

Silver born silver and other silvers born black, all appear much the same at maturity. Chinchilla is a cream with enough gray sprinkled in to give it the rather rare chinchilla color. This varies greatly depending on the length of the coat, but shows well where the coat has been trimmed short.

The black and tan pattern has been given different interpretations by geneticists. Some call the gene a pattern gene whereas others call it a modifying or saddle gene. It is associated with tan in most breeds and modifying genes determine the extent of the saddle which may vary from a small patch up to an almost all black dog so often seen in hounds which show only tan spots over the eyes and tan feet with some tan under the tail. In flat-coated, even long-haired dogs, this is an attractive color but in fuzzy haired dogs where there is a problem of lack of definition caused by the colors mixing, the black and tan is not so desirable.

Poodle breeding is made fascinating by what seem at times to be unpredictable results. What has given the greatest substance to this claim of unpredictability is such results as when a white Poodle has been mated to an apricot and produced over three litters: black, apricot, white, black and tan, blue and silver puppies. The uncertainty simply comes from not knowing the genetic background of the *apricot*. Two real whites can't produce any other color than white because white is recessive, but as we've seen, an apricot can carry quite a varied assortment of genes,

Geneticists have given us these insignia (initials) or names for the color genes. Remember that the capital letters represent dominant genes, the small letters, recessive, and that genes are always in pairs.

A – Colored all over – often called self colored
a – Spotted
B – Black
b – Brown, an inhibition gene
C – Colored – any color
c – Pink eyed albino
D – Intensely pigmented
d – Dilution gene, makes black, blue
E – Extension of the pigment in hairs
e – Restriction of hair pigment, producing cream and apricot
G – Greying which changes colors to black or silver
g – Absence of greying gene

How may one know the genetic constitution of any Poodle? By knowing the colors of the ancestors, by knowing what colors the parents have produced and by genetic testing which means mating the dog to dogs of several other colors and observing in what colors his or her puppies come.

When you pair two recessives, you'll get only puppies like their parents. There are blacks with BB constitution which never produce any other color puppies unless both parents carry a dilution gene which when paired with another produces blue puppies.

With the above information the reader will get a fairly good idea of the possibilities inherent in any mating when the genetic make-up of the parents is known. When it is not, surprise, surprise!

The Stud

Many people go to a show, pick out a dog they like, and decide that he is to be the mate for their female. He may be the right dog, but again he may not. A safer method is to write to owners of various likely studs and ask for details of their breeding, and compare these with your own bitch's pedigree. You will usually get better puppies if you keep to your own line, that is, mate your bitch to a dog who has some of the same forebears.

Another way is to go to as many shows as you can, and check the quality of puppies sired by the stud dog that takes your fancy. You can certainly expect to get a good litter by using a dog who is already siring good quality puppies now appearing in the ring, and who has himself a sound background of show winning ancestors. Often a very handsome dog is somewhat of a fluke, and although lovely himself, he will not produce puppies of anything like his own quality. A dog who is, however, able to reproduce his own superlative qualities in the majority of his offspring is known as a "prepotent sire" and is worth his weight in gold. This applies equally to a brood bitch. So, primarily, study his progeny that have already appeared when choosing your sire.

Another help towards the right choice is to select a dog who is particularly strong in the points in which your brood bitch is lacking. For instance, if she has a rather poor head, choose a dog with a long, lean head; or if her pigmentation is weak, then choose a dog that has jet black points, and throws puppies with jet black points. If your bitch is poor in coat, go for the dog with the magnificent coat, provided always that he does throw quality puppies, that his pedigree ties in with the pedigree of your bitch, and that he and his forebears have had their share of show prizes.

The Mating

Having made your choice, you should contact the owner of the dog, and make a provisional reservation for his service. As soon as your bitch comes in season, telephone the stud dog owner and make definite arrangements for taking your bitch to him. When you arrive, ask to see the dog and give him a going over, noting whether he appears alert and in good bright health, and whether he is absolutely clean underneath.

The owner of the stud may wish to take the bitch away from you for the actual mating, as sometimes the fact of a stranger being present can put off a dog at just the crucial moment and, too, bitches often behave a great deal better away from their owners. But you should ask to see them both as soon as the mating has been achieved, and while they are still "tied" – the tieing process lasts anywhere from ten to forty minutes. It is your right as the bitch's owner to see that this is going on, to check that the right dog has been used, and to reassure your own bitch while she waits for her release,

An ideal mating is one in which the bitch takes readily to the dog, and a good "tie" results; nevertheless, some excellent litters are produced when there has been no tie at all, and the mating has been completed in a few seconds instead of the usual half hour or so.

A young maiden bitch will usually do better if mated to an older and more experienced dog; a bitch who is getting on in years will do well with a younger one. The owner of the stud dog should give you the pedigree and the mating certificate when you pay the stud fee. If, by any chance, the mating proves unfruitful, most stud owners are perfectly willing to mate the bitch free of charge at her next season, although, strictly speaking, they are not bound to do this. Usually this question is brought up and agreement reached at the time the initial mating is being arranged. The stud dog, if he is a proved sire, has fulfilled his part of the contract; a free service is plainly a courtesy on the part of the owner of the dog.

If you cannot take your bitch to the dog, and wish to send her by train or air, send her in a good traveling box, and see that she travels in a collar with her lead fastened to the box, but not to her collar. Give the owner of the stud dog exact details of the time of her arrival and the station or airport, and it is wise to mark the box "Bitch in season, please do not let out". You should include the cost of her return trip when paying the stud fee.

If, on the other hand, you own the stud dog, and a bitch is coming to visit him, be sure that he is clean in coat, well-groomed, and in a really fit and healthy condition for a mating. An owner of a bitch, paying a stud fee, is entitled to expert treatment, and it is not good enough to put the two dogs together in a room or a yard house and hope for the best. You must know how to manage a mating if you have a stud dog at public stud, and if you do not know how to assist the dog, or have not yet learned, it would be advisable to get an experienced breeder to supervise the first couple of matings. A stud dog can easily injure himself, and also the bitch, unless there is some knowledgeable person present to prevent either dog from pulling away when the couple are tied, or to keep the bitch from turning around and biting the dog.

When the mating is complete, the stud dog should be sponged down underneath with a mild disinfectant, and then returned to his quarters and allowed to rest for at least an hour. It is inadvisable to feed either the dog or the bitch for three hours before or after a mating. A young stud dog can have his first mating at about ten months, and two more when about thirteen months; at approximately fifteen months he can go straight ahead with regular studs whenever required. Don't forget that if a dog is being used at stud he must have a good nourishing diet.

In special circumstances, the owner of the stud dog may agree to take the pick of the litter of puppies in lieu of the payment of a stud fee. In this case, the bitch would have be deemed suitable in pedigree, temperament and condition, and would also have to be a "proved" breeder. A maiden bitch is not usually acceptable for an arrangement of this type.

The Brood Bitch

Turning to the brood bitch, here again you will need to consider well before investing in a suitable specimen. It has often been said, "Oh, she's no good for show, but she'll do for breeding". A more short-sighted policy has never been voiced! You should *only breed from the best* if the quality of Poodles is to be kept high. Don't breed from faulty, unsound females – or, if you must, then try hard to eradicate these faults by choosing a suitable stud dog one who does not have these same faults and who will be able to improve the quality of the puppies. But remember, the stud dog cannot do more than half, and to breed really good puppies, both stud dog and brood bitch should be of the highest quality possible. A very high aim at which to strive is to try always to breed puppies that are just a little bit better in quality than their parents. So, purchase the soundest female you can. Try to choose one that has a background of easy whelping in her forebears, one from parents that have always bred strong, healthy puppies.

The first estrum or "heat" can occur at any time after the bitch is six months old, but it can vary. The large Standard Poodle may well come into heat just after six months of age, and the Miniature usually between eight and ten months, but the tiny Toy Poodle often does not commence her first heat until she is over a year old.

The signs that a bitch is coming into her season follow a regular pattern. She will begin to notice male dogs with interest, and begin to urinate more frequently. The vulva will begin to swell and blood will flow; but it may be several days before the flow of blood is obvious. To be quite sure that you know the day this flow begins, test her each morning with a piece of cotton. When a faint smear of blood is seen, count it as the first day of "heat". The flow will continue for about ten days, sometimes profusely, sometimes scantily. Then the color will fade to a pale pink, and the vulva will appear more swollen and a great deal softer.

It is generally agreed that a bitch is in perfect condition for a successful mating between the 10th and 13th day of her season. A test of her keenness for the male may be made by touching her at the back, and if ready for mating she will usually wave her tail from side to side. If she is a maiden bitch – that is, one who has not had puppies before – two matings are desirable, the second one 24 hours after the first. The gestation period, the time she is carrying her puppies, is 61 days, but Poodles often seem to have their families a few days early, especially their first litters. The estrous cycle occurs about every six months, so you can expect the female Poodle to begin her second season six months after the *commencement*, not the end, of her first.

It is better to breed from a female at her second season; then she is usually about 14 months old. Many owners breed from a bitch twice running, and then rest her for a year. This is a matter of choice and depends on whether the bitch has a large or a small litter, and on her stamina.

When taking your bitch to the stud, see that she relieves herself before meeting him. She should be in an absolutely clean condition; it is not advisable to feed her within three hours of mating.

Let her rest for some hours after the mating, and beware of any strenuous exercise. After mating, you will still need to keep a careful watch on her until at least the 21st day of her season, as she is quite capable of getting out and mating again – this time the dog of *her* choice, and she will probably fancy the most out and out mongrel!

If, by any chance, you decide not to mate her during a particular season, and she gets out to an undesirable dog, you can take her to a veterinarian for an injection that will nullify the litter, any time up to 36 hours after mating. This injection will prolong her season for 21 days. Or you can wait until she has been pregnant for about three weeks or more, and have the veterinarian inject her with Malucidin which will cause the puppies to liquify and be resorbed without the slightest inconvenience to the bitch. Neither practice will interfere with her coming into her next heat normally, or of having normal puppies at the next litter.

When the puppies are born, don't forget to let the owner of the stud dog know as careful records of mating are kept.

Prenatal Care

A female does not need any special care for the first five weeks of her pregnancy, except that it will be wise to deworm her ten days after mating. Nearly all puppies are born infested, but worming the mother beforehand does seem to cut down on their possibility quite considerably.

Bitches will need an increased amount of food halfway through their pregnancy; give them about double their usual rations, but in two portions instead of the one large meal a day.

In good time decide where you want your bitch to have her puppies, and prepare her quarters. If you plan for her to have her litter in a whelping box, let her sleep in this for at least ten days before the expected date of whelping – she may have quite decided views on where *she* should whelp, but if you can get her used to your choice in advance, she will probably take to it quite happily, although in the end she is likely to prefer the middle of your bed to anywhere else!

Apart from your feeding and providing suitable whelping quarters, there is a psychological aspect of the pregnancy to be borne in mind, and this certainly has a great bearing on the breeding of temperamentally sound puppies. During her pregnancy, the bitch is highly vulnerable. For one thing, she becomes a thing apart to many of her kennel mates. She behaves a little differently and she doesn't smell quite right to them. They may, therefore, molest or worry her, so she must be protected. Also, she will move more slowly as she becomes heavier, and will not be able to run from any trouble with her former agility. During the latter half of her pregnancy she should be kept on leash while out walking, for she is liable to panic if other dogs threaten or even approach her. Likewise, as she approaches her time, do not allow her to jump or jump down from any height, as this can often lead to a miscarriage.

Feed her in the same place and at the same time each day. Punctuality is important during the last month. She will be increasingly hungry, and will "fuss" if feeding times are not regular. For the first week after she has littered, she may have to be given her dish of food actually in the bed. An attentive and conscientious mother, she will not want to leave her babies even to feed, so indulge her.

Her calls of nature will also need special attention. She may be taken short, causing an accident. She must not be scolded, because she simply cannot help it. She must not feel she is in disgrace. Anticipate the problem by putting newspaper beside her bed.

Again, after the puppies arrive, she will have to relieve herself at regular intervals, as she will be drinking a lot of fluids, but she must never be shut outside away from her puppies. She must know that she can return to them just as soon as she has relieved herself. If she is kept away from them even a couple of minutes, she will become upset and act quite panicky; this is not only bad for her temperamentally – it can affect her milk supply.

If she is very heavy in whelp, she will find it difficult to be comfortable while lying down, so make sure that she has a soft and comfortable bed, one which is large enough for her to lie out flat, with support for her back, in a quiet and secluded corner where she can peacefully brood on the prospect ahead!

Quite often pregnant Poodles suffer from "morning sickness" which occurs about 14 to 21 days after mating. Too, they may turn against all food or drink for as long as a week. This happens when the puppies are quickening. It is a most worrying time for the owner, but this anxiety must not be passed on to the Poodle.

This morning nausea and turning against food is in itself a happy sign, as it usually means that a healthy litter is on the way. Any sudden refusal of food during the last ten days of pregnancy is quite another matter, and may very well cause anxiety; it could point to the presence of a dead puppy. Veterinary advice should be sought.

The three sizes of Poodles all look alike. This had led to a great deal of intersize crossing, which is not always desirable. Mating a large dog to a small bitch does not usually cause whelping problems in the first generation, but it may in the second.

XVI Whelping a Litter

With your bitch pregnant, we must now pass on to the more practical aspects of whelping.

The Whelping Box

The matter of comfortable quarters is the first consideration. The brood bitch must have a place where she is safe from intruders and her too curious fellows, and this place should be warm and free from drafts. If a small room can be set aside for the expected

Preparing for the litter-bed, thermometer, wire enclosure, burlap protector and infra-red heat lamp all in position and ready.

BARBARA LOCKWOOD

family it will save a lot of trouble. If the expectant mother is a Standard Poodle, large and heavy, it would be advisable to obtain or make a large box probably three feet square with sides approximately eight or ten inches high. Fixed along the inside of each of the four sides should be a wooden rail one inch in diameter fixed about five inches from the floor of the box. This keeps the puppies from being squashed against the side of the whelping box by their heavy mother, for it provides a passageway all around the sides where they can crawl out of harm's way. With a Miniature Poodle bitch, since she is considerably lighter, such precaution is not necessary, and a similar box without the wooden rods, measuring approximately 18 to 20 inches square, is suitable. A fence of wire enclosing a total area of about four feet square is an added advantage. Or instead, the Poodle's own bed, provided it is a large enough, will be suitable until the puppies are three weeks old and start to roam. If the brood bitch is a tiny Poodle, then possibly a small circular plastic bed about 12 to 15 inches in diameter would be correct, or else a cardboard box with one side cut down to allow her to get out and in to her puppies. In this last case, a wire puppy run of approximately three feet by four feet would be suitable.

Bedding varies with circumstances, but neither wood shavings or hay are suitable. If it is for a large dog, either wheat straw or excelsior (wood wool) is good, with plenty of layers of newspaper on the floor. For smaller Poodles, in the house, probably excelsior, or blanket rugs are better.

198

"Sometimes I wonder whether it's worth it all!" Her puppy is only a few days old and the eyes have not yet opened. It is completely dependent on its mother.

Temperature Control

An infra-red lamp is a great asset, as whatever the temperature is outdoors or in the room, the area immediately below the lamp will remain at the heat you wish. It can be either decreased or increased by raising or lowering the lamp, which should be suspended above the whelping bed on a chain or wire. Such a lamp will, of course, increase the entire room temperature, so a thermometer should be kept in, or close to, the bed, and a reading taken from time to time. The temperature in the bed should be between 75° and 80° for the first three days in the lives of the puppies. It can then gradually be reduced by raising the lamp an inch a day until a moderate temperature of around 60° is achieved.

Advance Preparations

The gestation period, as we said, for a bitch is 61 days, but since many Poodles produce their puppies at least three days early, it is well to prepare the bitch a week in advance of her due date. It is unwise to worry her with too much bathing and clipping, but there are two things that must be done.

First, the hair on her belly must be clipped, so that the puppies will have no difficulty in finding the teats. If hair is left long, it is inclined to mat into hard balls of milk and hair. These are very unhygienic and after several days, they may completely prevent the puppies from feeding. At the same time, the hair around the anus and the vulva should be trimmed close.

Second, her nails should be cut moderately short, and in the interest of her eventual coat condition, the coat should have quite a lot tipped off. This depends on the length of the coat, but if it is a Long Lion Clip, then two or three inches could be taken off. By the time the puppies are ready to leave her, at six to seven weeks, the coat will have grown again, and, by then, again be in prime condition if she has been well and carefully fed throughout the period. The day before there are signs of birth, the bitch may have her belly washed with a bland shampoo and warm water, and her teats gently rubbed with olive oil to soften them.

Signs of Labor

Now it remains only to wait until the signs of beginning labor are evident. There are one or two pointers that will alert you. First, her temperature will usually fall from the normal of 101.5° to around 99°, and this is a very sure sign that puppies will appear within 24 hours. Another sign is the appearance of a thick clear mucous discharge from the vulva, and yet a third sign will be when she wishes to urinate at more frequent intervals.

Along with these signs, there will be certain temperamental changes, for within a few hours of the commencement of her labor, she may refuse all food and drink, and will wish to be alone and in a place that is dimly lit and out of the way. It is at this moment that she should be put into the quarters where she is to have her puppies. It will be realized that a wire fence encircling the actual bed is helpful. Plenty of newspaper should be laid on the floor, and she will almost certainly tear them up with great energy and vigor. She should not be kept from doing this as the vigorous exercise will help to bring the puppies along.

You will have notified your veterinarian some time before the expected birth, and now will probably want to phone him that labor is imminent, although it will not be necessary for him to visit you at this point in the proceedings.

Equipment

There are still several items to be prepared. For instance, a pair of scissors should be ready for immediate use, cotton and paper towels should be at hand, as well as several rough towels. A supply of suitable powdered substitute for bitch's milk should have been purchased in case it becomes necessary to feed the puppies.

The Story of Roxie

Roxie was the authors' pet Poodle. This is how she had her children.

Knowing that Poodles can produce their puppies five days or more before their due date, we had everything prepared for Roxie a full week ahead. The wire pen was in position, the bed was ready, and the infra-red lamp had been set up.

The pen measured 48 inches by 24 inches and was 24 inches high, with a small hinged door in one end. A rug had been draped around three sides to keep out any possible drafts. Several layers of newspaper had been spread on the floor. The bed was a plastic one with a foam rubber filling. This was comfortable and also hygienic, as it was washable.

The infra-red lamp was suspended from a hook in the ceiling, as described, and the warmth from the bulb was directed over the bed. A flat thermometer was laid in the bed about four inches above floor level, so that the approximate heat on Roxie's head or back could be checked at any time.

Roxie had had her coat tipped down quite considerably, and the hair had been clipped from her abdomen.

A rubber sheet, bath towels, cotton and a large roll of absorbent paper were all ready, as was a hypodermic syringe and a sterilized pair of scissors in case they were needed.

It must be interpolated that the majority of canine births are trouble free and easy. Often a female will whelp her litter entirely by herself, without help either from her owner or a veterinarian – in fact, often the first one knows of the whelping is to find a strong and healthy litter of wriggly, furry little newborn creatures with the mother justly proud of her efforts, having washed them and lined them up at the milk bar, with no fuss or bother at all.

However, we knew that the whelping we are telling you about would not be easy. Roxie was a Toy Poodle only 8½ inches high at

BARBARA LOCKWOOD

The onset of labor, with the bitch in the throes of the first contractions. It is best to notify the vet at this time so that he can be available if necessary.

BARBARA LOCKWOOD

BARBARA LOCKWOOD

The appearance of the water bag at the vulva suggests that the birth of the puppies is imminent.

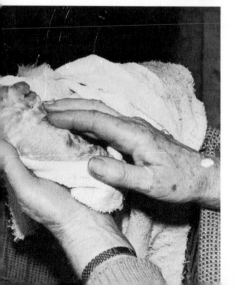

With the umbilical cord cut, the puppy is dried and massaged to encourage normal breathing.

the shoulder, and weighing only six pounds. She had been most carefully mated to a small dog who had only small breeding behind him. However, we would have been unusally lucky if the whelping of a Poodle the size of Roxie had gone without a hitch. It didn't. But we feel that all novice Poodle breeders should know how to cope with unusual problems if and when they occur, and that is why we are telling this true story.

Roxie was a little restless during the night, and demanded to be taken into the garden at 5 a.m. She then settled down to sleep again but woke at 7 a.m. and commenced to shiver. We took her temperature and found it to be 99°. We did not expect her to have her puppies for another five days, but at an earlier whelping she had given birth three days in advance of her due date so we were quite prepared for her to be just as early this time.

About one hour later, at 8 a.m., the first contraction was noticed and Roxie was in labor. Contractions were fairly mild to begin with, occurring regularly every ten minutes. The rubber sheet had been spread out and a thick bath towel laid on top, but Roxie soon had this in an untidy heap, spending a lot of time between contractions scratching and scraping at the towel. This was all to the good, we knew, as the more she moved about then, the easier her labor would be.

The veterinarian was phoned. We told him that everything was under control and that we would call again if assistance were required.

Time wore on, but by 10 a.m. nothing had occurred, except that the contractions were still occurring at regular intervals. We were glad to note that there was no lessening in the intensity of the straining. Any slackening would have given rise to anxiety, as it would probably have indicated that uterine inertia was on the way, and this usually ends in a Caesarian operation. However, we felt that Roxie should be showing more evidence of the arrival of her first puppy, so she was taken into the garden to walk around for a few minutes. This had the desired effect for within two minutes of returning to the whelping place, the water bag had made its appearance. This water bag resembles a balloon, about the size of a ping pong ball, protruding from the vulva. Uusally the first puppy arrives within ten to fifteen minutes after the appearance of the water bag, but this time we were not so lucky. However, at 11 a.m. a puppy could be seen in the neck of the vulva, and a few minutes later it

The puppy is about one minute old, and the mother is still wondering whether it was worth it all.

All's well that ends well! Ten minutes after birth, the puppy is being weighed for the record.

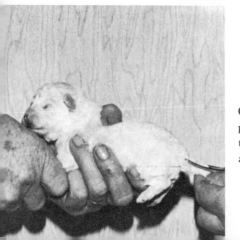

Cutting a ring of hair on the puppy's tail in preparation for the docking process. The scissors are blunt and curved.

was obvious that it was positioned right and would be presented head first. We were much relieved. After several more strong contractions, the puppy was born, struggling and wriggling to get out of the transparent sac in which it was enclosed. We tore a hole in the sac to let out the fluid and quickly freed the puppy's head, at the same time drying off the fluid inside its mouth with a corner of the towel.

The puppy was a lovely female with a lusty voice. She was, of course, still attached by the umbilical cord to the placenta, or afterbirth, which had not yet been evacuated by the mother. However, by gentle pulling, we drew out the placenta, and then cut the umbilical cord about three inches from the puppy's navel. The puppy was then put into a small cardboard box lined with towelling, which had been prepared in advance, and this was placed on a stool about two feet below the infra-red lamp, so that the puppy would have a heat radiation upon her of about 80° to 85°.

Roxie was a little exhausted and quite content to nap until the labor pains started again. In the meantime, the veterinarian telephoned, and we were happy to be able to tell him that everything was fine so far, and there were no complications. Normal contractions recommenced, and at 12:30 it was clear that the second puppy was presenting itself. This was obvious because the area surrounding the vulva was hard and lumpy, and the puppy was undoubtedly right there. But instead of a blunt puppy nose appearing, we could see that the presentation was backward, and a breech was to be expected.

Quite often this makes little difference with a Poodle, as they have fine, small heads. With some of the large headed breeds such as Pekingese, Pugs, Bulldogs, and so forth, a breech birth can give considerable trouble. But we could see two tiny hind feet protruding from the vulva, and unfortunately these seemed to be stuck, for they did not move down any farther. Had we been too quick in telling the veterinarian that all was well? Certainly this looked like real trouble. At each contraction, the two hind feet appeared, but as we tried to get a grip on them, they were drawn back into the vagina. The situation was full of danger, for obviously the membranous sac was punctured and the fluid had escaped. This meant that the puppy was no longer cushioned, and was liable to be badly bruised and crushed while actual parturition occurred. Should we call the veterinarian? Would he advise an immediate Caesarian?

In any case, it would be twenty minutes at least before he could arrive, and by that time the puppy would almost certainly be dead. What were we to do?

It was at this moment that we bitterly regretted having ever mated our tiny Poodle, and vowed that we would never breed another litter! But then – were the two legs protruding a fraction more, or was it our imagination? No, there was at least an inch, or perhaps even more, visible at the mouth of the vulva. With a clean linen handkerchief we were able to grasp the tiny feet, and each time the bitch strained we very gently pulled the tiny body down. It was difficult, and it took a long time. The pressure had to be so gentle, and yet each time we could see perhaps ⅛ of an inch more of the tiny body appearing. But there was still the head to get through the cervix! Would we be in time to save the puppy's life? After many minutes of anxious struggling, the puppy was at last pushed out – and there it lay, flacid, ivory white, and quite flat, and *also quite dead*.

Our disappointment was intense. There seemed no hope for him at all, but we quickly freed him from what was left of the sac, drew out the afterbirth, and severed the umbilical cord with our fingernails – there was no time to think of tying with thread and snipping with scissors. There was really no chance for him anyway, for there was no heart beat, no breathing. What could we do?

First, we swiftly wrapped him in a piece of towelling and held him fairly close to the lamp, rubbing his little back vigorously with our fingers. But he was quite lifeless, and there was no resistance in his little body. Then we turned him on his back and massaged his heart with two fingers. But he was still white, with no color in his nose, his gums or his toes. What about the Kiss of Life? It was a last chance. So he was held in an upright position and his mouth and nose were covered with the human mouth, and human breath was breathed into his lungs and breathed out again at a rate of approximately sixteen times a minute. This was continued for ten minutes, but with no result. Was there any point in continuing? It seemed not. Let's try just once more. The seconds dragged by. But surely that little ear twitched – or was it our imagination? Certainly that back leg gave a feeble kick! Don't stop now! Press on! Press on! And then the sound we had been longing to hear – the tiny chest expanded, the puppy's mouth opened wide, and he gave a sharp, shrill squeak. There was hope at last!

Again his heart was massaged vigorously; now his squeaks were becoming loud and continuous, and every second his breathing was approaching normal. Gradually his nose, his feet and his gums became a bright rose pink, and we knew we had won. He was alive and very much kicking! Our excitement was overwhelming. Within a short time he was able to join his sister on his mother's breast, and ten minutes later we found it quite a problem to tell them apart. The moral to this true story is never, never give up. You may save a valuable puppy even after half an hour of apparent lifelessness *if you try hard enough.*

We ourselves were completely exhausted and hot sweet tea would have been most welcome, but first the little mother had to be given sustenance, for after all, at this point, she needed stimulation more than anyone. So a warm drink of milk and glucose was prepared, and this she drank thirstily. The two puppies were put in the bed with her, and she settled down to a good sleep.

After an hour we satisfied ourselves that there were no more puppies to come. Gentle manual examination of her body told us this; moreover, Roxy was giving herself an energetic wash, and it is rare for a bitch to clean up if more puppies are on the way. She certainly was a littly messy, so we washed her tail and back parts with warm water, and then carefully dried her. While this was being done, the blanket was changed and the puppies settled on a clean one. It was not considered necessary to insist on Roxie's going out to relieve herself for several hours, and when she did, it was made easy for her to rush back to her precious babies without delay. But while she was out the opportunity was taken to weigh the puppies, for this information was needed for the records.

Roxie now needed several meals a day, and as she was such a devoted mother, these meals had to be given to her in bed, for she refused to leave her puppies even for food until they were more than two weeks old. So she was given a slightly warm milk drink at 6 a.m., a scrambled egg mixed with a little brown bread at 10 a.m., another milk drink at 2 p.m., and a good meal of raw meat at 6 p.m. After a day or so she preferred cooked meat to raw, and was given liver or fish for a change. Another milk drink was given at 10 p.m. For the first two nights a small drink of warm milk and glucose was given in the middle of the night. After this, nature asserted itself. Our tiny Toy regained her strength quickly and reared her babies uneventfully - an excellent mother.

An American Whelping

That is how it was with Roxie. We shall now contrast our procedure with an American one. This is how a New England Poodle breeder manages his whelpings.

He tells us that his Standards and Miniatures are kept in wire bottom pens with a hutch attached to each. When whelping time comes, he clips the bitches all over so that one would scarcely recognize them as Poodles. In winter he leaves an inch of coat; in summer he clips them closely.

His beds consists of dehydrated sugar cane, pressed into saucer shape so that the puppies roll into a pile in the bottom. When the mother moves about them to lie down, she gently pushes the babies into a pile and then lies down with her teats available to them. There are no rods around the periphery of the whelping box and his losses from bitches lying on puppies are insignificant.

All of the dogs are fed a good commercial food demonstrated to be complete. To this he adds fat which he buys from a butcher, ground through a hamburger grinder and chilled. The regular ration consists of 85% commercial food and 15% fat. After the bitches whelp, the fat is raised to 25% because this helps in the production of milk with its high fat content.

The bitches are carefully watched during the whelping to be certain that nothing is going wrong. Whelps are left with the mother, the exception being when the litters are very large. One of his Standard bitches whelped 12 pups and raised them all. In such cases, some of the puppies are stolen from the mother by covering her eyes with one hand and removing some of the puppies with the other. After the completion of whelping they are returned.

No artificial heat is ever used but of course the bitches are used to the outside temperature of the kennels. They often whelp in winter when the temperature is well below freezing, without losing a puppy. In the cold weather a burlap cloth is hung over the entrance of the hutch. The newborn puppies are licked nearly dry by their mothers and they nestle closely to her and keep so warm they soon dry off.

Poodles are as rugged dogs as those of any breed and can cope with low temperatures provided they are acclimated gradually and are not clipped short during the cold months. Owners of personal, pampered Poodles would not and should not subject them to rugged winter weather after they have been used to the warmth of heated homes. This would be cruel. We cite the above to show you that it is not at all necessary to fuss with Poodles any more than we would with dogs of other breeds.

Cleaning the Puppies

The bitch usually attends to the cleaning of the puppies, and no evidence of the feces they have passed is found in the bed. She will continue to clean them until weaning commences, but as soon as any food other than mother's milk is given, she will discontinue her cleaning duties and pass the responsibility over to you. You must then watch that the puppies do not become soiled behind. If this does happen, the clogged hair must be carefully cut away, the anus washed with warm water and a little soothing ointment applied.

Docking Tails and Removing Dewclaws

When the puppies are nearing seven weeks old, the tails will have to be docked, and the dewclaws removed. A novice will want the veterinarian to do this, but if you decide to breed Poodles regularly, you will probably want to learn how to do the job yourself.

Take the bitch away from the puppies, completely out of earshot. It will upset her very much if she hears the cry of the puppies and cannot get to them. There are two methods employed for docking tails, amputation or by rubber band.

The authors prefer the rubber band method, as this causes the puppies the minimum of pain, and they appear to recover immediately afterwards, whereas after amputation there is constant crying and grizzling for a number of hours. The procedure is to snip off a ring of hair around the tail at the point at which it is to be docked. It is well to err on leaving a longer tail than a too short one, since a Poodle loses all his elegance if his tail is too short. Take the smallest size rubber band and (one about ½-inch in diameter) and slip it over the end of the tail on to where you have snipped the ring. Stretch the band, twist it, and put around the tail again - continue stretching, twisting and putting around the tail until the rubber band is *very tight* indeed, in fact, tight enough to completely stop the circulation of the blood. The puppy will give a cry at the last two twists and will then appear to feel no more pain. The tiny end will soften and wilt after 24 hours, and at the end of two or three

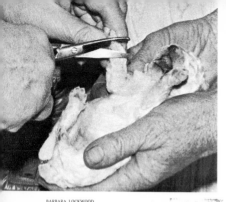

The author recommends taking the puppies to the veterinarian to have their dewclaws removed before they are a week old. This is the position in which the puppy is held and the angle of the curved scissors used in removing dewclaws.

BARBARA LOCKWOOD

weeks drop off, leaving a nicely healed pink end to the tail.

If amputation is employed, tie a piece of very narrow bandaging tightly around the tail above where it is planned to cut, to stop the circulation. The unwanted end of tail is then sharply cut off with a pair of sterilized scissors, and a blood clotting agent applied to the raw end at once. It is essential to watch the puppy for an hour or so in case of renewed bleeding. It is also *essential* to remove the bandage ligature within eight hours of the amputation. It should be snipped through with a pair of sharp scissors.

Some breeders use no ligature but simply snip off the tail. If the bleeding is excessive, do not return the pup to the mother until the blood flow stops and healing begins. Many a bitch has licked the stump of the tail so much that she prevented healing.

Dewclaws may appear on front feet; they resemble an unwanted thumb. Occasionally they are also present on the hind feet; all must be removed. Hold the puppy's paw tightly with the finger and thumb of the left hand, to stop circulation of the blood, and with the right hand snip out the dewclaw with a pair of sharp curved scissors. Be sure that a deep enough cut is made so that the root of this extra claw is removed. If only a superficial cut is made, the dewclaw will grow again. Immediately after cutting, and while still holding the little paw, press permanganate of potash crystals (or some other blood clotting and cauterizing agent) into the wound, making sure that no bleeding now takes place.

At the same time, and afterwards regularly once a week, cut the sharp tips of the nails on the forefeet because they can prick the bitch when she is feeding the puppies, hurting her. If this is neglected, a bitch may turn on her puppies, or suddenly refuse to feed them.

There is no doubt that you will get a tremendous lift from the litter of puppies, but they will also prove to be great timewasters! What a rewarding way to waste time!

Weaning the puppy! An anxious mother watches to be sure that it's done properly.

XVII   Weaning the Puppies

The next stage in the puppy's life is the weaning process. It is difficult to be precise as to when this should occur for it depends on the dam's milk supply, and on the size of the litter. It can be as early as three weeks, or as late as seven or eight. But the usual sign that the puppies need extra food is when they begin to snuffle around her dish, or begin to suck the ears or legs of the other puppies in the litter.

Frequently, the bitch will take the matter into her own hands, and regurgitate her own food for the puppies. If she decides to throw up her dinner for the babies, don't imagine that she is being sick and quickly clean up the mess. Let the puppies have it, for it is the best possible weaning food, being, as it is, predigested. But when this happens, give the mother food which is either minced or cut very small, food which is, in fact, suitable for handing on to her puppies – and don't forget to give her a second dinner for her own!

Apart from this regurgitated food (and not all bitches do regurgitate) the puppies may have two milky drinks each day.

For their first meal smear some margarine on the bottom of a saucer and let the youngsters lap it. Put no more than an eighth of an inch of light cream in the saucer, and they will lap this. Do not put so much cream that they can dunk their noses or they may inhale some and become afraid of the food. When they have learned to lap this cream, make the amount deeper each feeding until they can lap without inhaling it.

Gradually add some solid puppy food and make a gruel, giving less cream, because the puppy food will supply all the essentials, only needing warm water to make it palatable. Don't overfeed but feed regularly at the same times. Increase the amounts as they grow bigger. Watch the stools for diarrhea or constipation. See that they have a bowl of cold fresh water from the age of about four weeks onward. With this routine you should experience no difficulty.

While the puppies are being weaned, separate them from the mother for increasingly longer periods, until they do not feed from her all day, and then, finally, remove her at night as well. Always remember that this is a difficult time for her; she may well cling to her puppies and be "difficult" over giving them up. When she has to be taken away from them, provide her with another interest, such as a ride with you in the car, or a walk in the park, or a large and succulent bone to gnaw.

The time will come when the puppies will move on to different homes. In another chapter hints are given on preparing a puppy for sale. But if it is possible, arrange it so that all the puppies are not taken away from the mother at the same time. If they all leave at once, it can cause her great mental stress and anxiety, and becomes a very poor reward when she has bred you a nice and valuable litter. Try to arrange that one or perhaps two leave her on one day, and the rest a week later, or by gradual stages. It is the last puppy that will cause her the most heartache, and by then she must have as many different interests to divert her attention as you can possibly arrange.

Building up the Mother

Once the puppies have been weaned, the mother's stamina should be built up. So often when puppies leave the dam, her food is automatically cut down, the general notion being that she doesn't need so much now. This is a shortsighted policy, and if you expect her to breed well for you again, she must have special attention at this juncture.

She will certainly not need so much food in *quantity* but she must have food of *extra quality* so that the strong body condition she lost while rearing a litter may be built up again.

If her regular ration is complete, one you can trust, continue feeding it. She may eat a little more than you might expect as she stores reserves after having suckled her litter. Remember that a bitch on an inadequate diet, especially one with insufficient calcium has withdrawn calcium from her reserves in her bones and teeth. It often happens that bitches have eclampsia while they are lactating, demonstrating that their diet is incomplete. That occurs most frequently in bitches that have been fed mostly on muscle meat which has almost no calcium. In diets concocted at home, it may even be necessary to add vitamins and minerals to keep bitches healthy. But if a sound commercial diet is fed, calcium, being one of the least expensive ingredients, is almost always present abundantly. So are other essential minerals and vitamins. So if you want your brood bitch to regain her former condition with the least possible delay, and

A tiny Poodle still in the nest. See the glossy waves in the coat and the snug set of the ears even at this early age. When he grows up he'll be a beauty!

SALLY ANNE THOMPSON

to be sure that she produces an equally satisfactory litter the next time, take great care over building her up as soon as she has given up her puppies.

Hand Rearing a Litter

It is hoped that this may never become necessary because it is a difficult and onerous task. The fact must be faced, however, that it occasionally happens that the mother may not produce any milk and therefore cannot feed her offspring, or that she may die giving birth to the puppies. It is not common occurrence, but it is essential to know what to do should it happen.

If the mother has no milk, but is able to wash and clean her puppies, the task is not too difficult. But if the puppies are left motherless, you will have to attend to all their needs, and this will indeed keep you busy.

First and foremost, the puppies must be fed at very regular intervals in a carefully prepared schedule. Three hourly feeding intervals, day and night, are essential for the first seven days; then it may be possible to reduce them to six hour intervals. Temperature of the milk is a most important point, and this should be blood heat, or approximately 101°. If a large litter is being hand reared, there is a danger that the milk food will have become too cool by the time the last puppy is fed. To obviate this, the cup or bottle containing the food should be stood in a vessel of hot water to keep the temperature more or less even.

Some breeders use a baby's bottle with a premature teat, but the authors have always found a glass eye dropper more satisfactory. The food should be freshly prepared for each feed, and a milk preparation specially formulated to resemble the constituents of bitches' milk should be used. If it is impossible to obtain this, a formula intended for human babies will do, but it must be remembered that bitches' milk is far stronger than cows' milk, containing as it does almost three times the amount of fat, ten times the amount of albumin, and twice the amount of solids. From this it will be seen that a food which compares as much as possible to the milk of a healthy bitch must be looked for. Breeders sometimes dilute cows' milk for puppies, erroneously thinking it is too strong for them. In fact, it is quite the reverse, as the following table of comparisons will show:

	Fat	Casein	Albumin	Milk Sugar	Ash	Total Solids	Water
Cow	3.73	3.04	0.54	4.90	0.71	12.92	87.08
Bitch	9.57	6.10	5.05	3.08	0.73	24.53	75.47
Goat	4.78	3.20	1.09	4.46	0.76	14.29	85.71
Cat	3.33	3.12	5.93	4.91	0.58	17.90	82.10

Many tiny Toy Poodles have been nursed by cats, and certainly seem to flourish well. Cats are the most devoted mothers, and puppies reared by them always have superlative coats, due no doubt to the rough and "scratchy" tongues of cats, who seem to be continually licking and grooming their adopted children.

Another important point is not to overfeed the newborn puppy. Half a teaspoonful of fluid at a time is enough for a feed for a Toy Poodle for the first seven days, a little more for a Miniature puppy, and double that quantity for a Standard. This means approximately three (or six for Standard puppies) pipettes or droppersful. The method is to hold the puppy in your left hand, either in cotton or a small piece of blanket, in an upright position, and then gently press the nozzle of the dropper into the puppy's mouth. Very slowly press the rubber cap or bulb on the end, so that the puppy receives a drop or two at a time. After the first few feeds, the puppy will know exactly what to do, and the fluid will be quickly sucked down.

If there is no mother to attend to the cleaning of the puppies, you must do it for her. Normally the mother stimulates the puppy to urinate and defecate by licking him. A puppy will not survive unless he regularly empties his bowels and his bladder, and so he must be *made* to do this. Have a small bowl of warm water available, soak a small piece of cotton and slightly squeeze it out. Then, with the puppy lying in your hand on his back, gently stroke the prepuce or vulva with the warm, damp cotton; the puppy will immediately pass water. Keep on stroking until he has finished. The same procedure is carried out on the anus, and although it takes a little longer, you must persevere until feces are passed. This procedure must be followed after every single meal, if the puppies are to remain healthy. If they become a little sore, a smear of white Vaseline, or zinc and castor oil ointment should be administered.

In the case of motherless puppies, it is necessary to keep them very

Three marvelous Miniatures. Silver Poodles are born black, a silver color gradually coming in as they mature.

warm. To this end, an infra-red lamp is almost essential, as any great variation in temperature will cause chills and diarrhea.

Puppies that are hand reared are usually able to lap much sooner than those raised normally. You can expect such a puppy to lap from a shallow dish at 2 to 2½ weeks of age. It goes without saying that all feeding containers, pipettes, spoons, and so forth, must be kept scrupulously clean if upset stomachs are to be avoided.

Hand reared puppies, of course, miss out on valuable colostrum, which is the first fluid produced by the bitch. This fluid contains globulin which, as we saw provides the puppies with antibodies to immunize them against disease for the first seven or eight weeks of their lives. Hence, puppies who are deprived of colostrum must be given other means of immunization in the form of gamma globulin; the veterinarian will advise you on this.

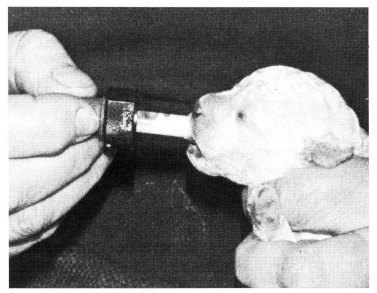

An important point is not to overfeed the newborn puppy. Three or four droppersful at a time is enough of a meal for a Miniature puppy.

Puppies for sale; and who could resist them?

Love for sale!

Puppies for Sale

The final act when rearing a litter of Poodles is to prepare them for sale and for their new homes. Of course, you *can* sell your puppies as woolly, somewhat unkempt, little ragamuffins who might be any breed – perhaps Sealyham or Wire Fox Terrier. On the other hand, you can take a little trouble and prepare your puppies so that they are clean, groomed, unquestionably resembling well-bred Poodles. If you do this, your puppies will command a better price, and the purchaser will be getting better value for his money.

Most Poodle puppies leave home when eight to ten weeks old. Before they are presented for inspection to would-be purchasers, they should be carefully shampooed in a bland, pure shampoo, and carefully dried and groomed. They should also be given their first Puppy clip, which means clipping the hair from the face, feet and base of tail. It is advisable to leave on a small moustache, for many buyers do not like a clean shaven face. One can always clip off an unwanted moustache, but one cannot put it back!

The sharp tips of the nails on all four feet must be nipped off. The puppies should have already been given their first worming.

All registration papers should be in order, ready to hand to the new owner, together with the puppy's pedigree and a diet sheet carefully outlining the meals that he is currently used to.

And so we have completed the full circle in the life of the Poodle. Poodles are certainly an absorbing hobby, whether we fancy the breeding of puppies, the showing of the breed, or obedience training – or just want to have a few around the home for good companions.

Junior competitors take their shows very seriously.
Courtesy of Mrs. Marlene Scott, the judge shown here.

English Champion Oakington Puckshill Ambersunblush, shown after winning Supreme Best in Show at Cruft's in 1966. In order to do this, she had to win over 7,773 of all breeds. Owned by Mrs. Paul Perry and bred by Mrs. Myles Dobson.

An outdoor ramble is lots of fun.. However, always examine your Poodle carefully afterwards to make sure he hasn't picked up any foreign matter or intruders. Pay particular attention to his pads, ears, eyes and coat.

XVIII   Health of the Poodle

We hope that the Poodle you have chosen will be a healthy dog, and it is more than likely that he will be, since, as a breed, they are far from delicate. However, the threat of disease is always in the mind of dog owners, particularly in these days when new viruses are constantly being identified. Their existence has been known since the 19th century, but only in recent times has it been possible to investigate the actual nature of the virus organism. And while there is an increased number of viruses that attack dogs, there are also many more means of protecting the dog against their onslaught.

Colostrum

The first protection a puppy receives against disease is from a substance called colostrum, which reaches him through his mother's milk during the first few days of his life. This colostrum gives immunity against many diseases and protects the puppy until he is between eight and twelve weeks old. At that age, the immunity grows weak, and the puppy gradually becomes less protected against disease. Puppies that for some reason have missed out on their mother's milk, and have been hand reared, will not have received this natural immunity, and they are thus wide open to any infection. Such puppies should be inoculated with gamma globulin at birth as this will provide the necessary antibodies to fight infection.

Inoculations

When the natural immunity begins to fade, the puppy must be vaccinated with one or more of the special vaccines evolved to protect dogs from such diseases as Hard Pad, Distemper, Contagious Hepatitis and Leptospirosis. However, vaccination has little or no effect if it is done while the puppy has, in its blood stream, a high level of antibodies derived from its mother. Because of this, puppies are not usually vaccinated against Distemper and Hepatitis until they are about twelve weeks old. However, there are times when the veterinarian may decide that another age is safer, or may even strongly advise a second vaccination shortly after the first.

The vaccination against Hepatitis usually gives complete protection for the duration of the dog's life, but in the case of Distemper and Hard Pad a "booster" inoculation is advised every year. Discuss it with your veterinarian – it is so much better to be safe than sorry.

Distemper, Hepatitis, Leptospirosis

But in spite of all the preventive care taken, virus diseases do occur. The three main ones are Distemper, Hepatitis and Leptospirosis, and, as the symptoms are sometimes similar, it is difficult to know exactly which virus is attacking and it can only be isolated by a veterinarian after observation. Usually the first symptoms in all of these diseases are a sudden rise in temperature (but this may last only a few hours, and then drop to normal). The next ones may be a sudden loss of appetite and turning away from all food; sneezing and the production of a thick yellow mucus from the nostrils; eyes which are "deep" and cloudy, with blobs of yellow mucus in the corners; intermittent shivering, and tendency to tuck up closely and sleep, although the sleep may be fitful and restless. These symptoms will shortly be followed by nausea and diarrhea.

Whenever these signs are noticed, the puppy should be immediately isolated from all other dogs and puppies. He must be kept warm, and his temperature checked and recorded twice a day. When the disease is really taking hold, the temperature will start to rise, reaching 105°, or even higher, from the norm of 101.5°. But it cannot be stressed too often or too strongly that the sooner veterinary help is obtained, the better are your Poodle's chances. There are many antibiotics in use today which will help considerably in fighting disease, but if a virus has been allowed to multiply without treatment, the outlook is less than hopeful.

Before The Doctor Comes

So, if your dog shows any of these symptoms, isolate him in a warm, quiet place where there is not too much light; give him nothing at all to eat until the veterinarian has examined him. Some nourishment that will do no harm is a heaping teaspoonful of honey in water.

As these diseases take their course, other symptoms become apparent, giving more definite proof of which virus is attacking. In Distemper or Hard Pad, typical symptoms are the puppy's sensitivity to light, for he will wish to close his eyes against light, and hide in dark places. Another typical pointer is the temperature which flies up on the first day of the attack, then reverts to normal, only to rise even higher after two or three days. There it will remain for from 10 to 20 days according to the severity of the attack. There is often a crop of yellow-headed spots or pustules on the stomach, the breath is particularly foul and acrid, and there is usually a dry, husky cough. The incubation period for Distemper and Hard Pad is five days.

The symptoms of Hepatitis, a disease that attacks the liver, are slightly different. Unfortunately, its onslaught is so swift that a puppy may die before it is diagnosed, or treatment given. However, if the dog survives the first 48 hours, he has a good chance of

To administer liquids, pull the lips out gently to form a small "pocket." Raise the dog's head so that the liquid will run down his throat.

SALLY ANNE THOMPSON

recovery. The whites of the eyes will often be bloodshot, while the cornea will become light blue and opaque. Often the puppy may be temporarily blind. There is not the same possibility of ultimate brain damage as with Distemper.

The third gruesome disease is Leptospirosis, often referred to as Infectious Jaundice. It is a disease spread by rats and dogs who contaminate drinking water with their urine. In Leptospirosis there is great weakness and constant vomiting. To begin with, the temperature drops to sub-normal, and the dog is exceedingly depressed and lethargic. There is tremendous thirst, and stiffness of the limbs. The whites of the eyes, and the tongue and lips take on a yellow tinge. The incubation period is between five and fourteen days.

Kennel Cough

An especially troublesome mild disease which often runs rampant through kennels is characterized by a constant hacking cough. It is thought to be the result of a virus infection in the upper respiratory tract. In effect, it makes puppies difficult to sell because buyers are not content with the explanation that the puppy will surely recover and thenceforth be immune. Rather the buyer is suspicious of Distemper or Hepatitis.

There are drugs which your veterinarian can supply which will alleviate the irritation and lessen the cough. After a few weeks the body builds up resistance and the dog recovers spontaneously.

223

Kennel cough is often mistaken for roundworm or hookworm infestation. A heavy infection of coccidia often produces similar symptoms.

Colds

Dogs may occasionally suffer from colds, or Rhinitis, but these are not caused by the virus which attacks humans, nor can colds be transmitted from dog to human, or vice versa. A dog suffering from Rhinitis sneezes constantly for a couple of days; he will weep and produce a clear discharge from his nose. It is highly infectious from dog to dog, but not too serious.

Diarrhea

Diarrhea is a condition commonly referred to as an illness, but this is not correct. Diarrhea, in itself, is simply nature's way of ridding the dog of impurities. The very fact that the dog has Diarrhea is itself a good sign, for it means that he is getting rid of the poisons, impurities or whatever, that are upsetting him. The worst thing for Diarrhea is the administration of a chalky "stopping-up" medicine which simply acts as a "cork"; this allows the impurities to spread through the dog's system. In itself, Diarrhea is of no account, but as it may herald some serious disease, professional advice should be sought if it does not clear up in 24 hours, particularly so if there is an accompanying rise in temperature. In puppies it often is caused by coccidiosis.

Constipation

Diet is usually to blame. Give your dog something else to eat. Provide more vegetables and roughage like kibble and dog biscuits. For fast relief, use milk of magnesia – a child's dose; or, if you prefer, olive oil straight or mixed in with his food. When the situation has been corrected, continue the new diet; otherwise the condition may reappear. Feed a soft, bland diet, easily digested until the symptoms have passed. Many veterinarians recommend feeding, when a dog is not well, equal amounts of chopped meat and rice mixed together with the addition of 10 percent canned stewed tomatoes. This should be fed as the sole diet until the dog is normal.

Lesser Ailments

There are, of course, other serious ailments which attack dogs; for example, Bronchitis, Gastritis, heart disease, poisoning, Diabetes and many others, but these almost always require professional diagnosis. However, you should be able to recognize any unusual behavior immediately. If your dog suddenly goes off his food, or wants to drink excessively, or has constant spasmodic fits of shivering, if he is unusually sleepy and constantly tucks himself up into an unwakeable ball, this should flash you the red light. Obviously something is not quite right, and you should immediately check his temperature and his pulse. If not close to normal, call the veterinarian without delay.

Many illnesses need only be mild ones if an owner is quick to spot anything of the ordinary. On the other hand, owners with little perception or powers of observation may not notice that the Poodle is ill until symptoms are far advanced and possibly out of control.

Worms

There are four common types of worms: whipworms, roundworms, tapeworms, and hookworms. Both hookworms and roundworms attack puppies. Hookworms resemble short pieces of white cotton thread, and roundworms are pinkish-white in color, round and very much resemble short lengths of spaghetti. They are usually tightly coiled when eliminated.

The usual symptoms in a puppy harboring these worms are diarrhea, the stool having a somewhat jellified consistency, and, sometimes, a voracious appetite, though often a poor one. The puppy's breath may be unpleasant, and he may "scoot" about, dragging his behind along the floor. And, of course, the obvious symptom of passing the worms or vomiting them.

In adult Poodles, the same symptoms apply; in addition, the eyes may be dull and the coat flat and lifeless. Puppies should be dosed for worms as soon as they are demonstrated. A second worm dose should be given if necessary 11 days after the first; thereafter, when necessary. Nowadays, with modern drugs, it is not necessary to starve the dog before dosing. Ask the veterinarian for the correct dose, as he must consider the dog's breed, age and weight.

Tapeworms are more serious, and they are distinctly unpleasant; adult dogs, rather than puppies, are usually infected. A tapeworm can be several feet in length; it looks like a length of cream-colored tape or ribbon, with a head at one end and a tapered tail at the other.

Often a dog suffering from tapeworm will have segments of the worm (which resemble grains of rice) adhering to the hair around the anus or in his stools. Dogs usually pick up tapeworms from fleas, and sometimes rabbits, for there must be an intermediary host. The dog cannot "catch" worms from another dog. The flea or rabbit harbors the tapeworm cysts; the Poodle eats the flea or the rabbit, and the tapeworm cysts hatch out in the Poodle, the head adhering to the intestine and segments growing from the head.

A Poodle suffering from tapeworms has a dull and lifeless coat, dull eyes, indifferent appetite, and there is a typical and unpleasant odor in both breath and skin. The veterinarian must be consulted to prescribe the correct vermifuge and dosage.

While not as common as the others, whipworms are harder to detect. They are found more frequently in warmer climates since the eggs are incubated in warm soil. The worms are about two inches long, but their diameter is no more than that of coarse thread. They attach themselves to the dog's intestines and cecum – a blind pouch in the intestinal tract. Severe infestation can produce anemia, fits and,

The Eggs of Four Common Worms

Toxocara canis, Roundworm.   *Dipylidium caninum*, Tape worm,

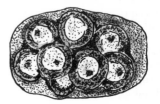

Trichuris vulpis, Whip worm,   *Ancylostoma caninum*, Hook worm.

CHET PLEGGE, D.V.M.

226

in extreme cases, death. *Symptoms:* Loss of appetite, staring coat, eye discharge. *Treatment:* N butyl chloride is usually given, but this should be undertaken only by a vet.

Skin Ailments

Slow, rhythmic scratching in one particular place (or places) indicates a skin infection or irritation. Examine the dog carefully, parting the coat with a comb, until you discover those spots where the skin is bare or inflamed. There are several brands of antiseptic powder which help to alleviate simple skin disorders. You may want to try one of these if the ailment is in its early stage; but as skin complaints spread rapidly, have a variety of causes, and are notoriously hard to cure, my recommendation is to seek professional advice and save yourself, not to mention the dog, a long and trying experience.

Ringworm

Ringworm is not a worm at all but a fungus which attacks dogs and cats as well as human beings. It can be passed back and forth from animals to man. Sores appear more often on the ears, face, neck, and tail than on other parts of the body. Since the hair is not shed, the infected areas may be overlooked for some time. As the infection spreads, the patches get larger and become incrusted.
Treatment: Cut away the hair from the lesions, remove the incrusted material with mineral oil and a cotton swab and apply a recommended ringworm cure. Sometimes tincture of iodine will bring it under control. Since ringworm can be caught by humans, it is advisable to seek professional help and to wear gloves and be especially careful when treating the animal. Never let a child play with a dog suffering from ringworm, or vice versa.

Eczema

This, a common skin ailment, is sometimes mistaken for ringworm or mange. It seems to have a number of causitive agents-allergy, fungi, fleas, and chiggers as well as faulty diet. It is characterized by intense itching, dandruff, loss of hair, sores and scabs. There are two types, moist and dry, with the most more often affecting the Poodle. *Treatment:* Wash the affected parts with soap and water – a medicated soap like Dial is good, and apply a recommended lotion or ointment. Chronic cases should be turned over to the vet.

Mange

There are several types of mange. If you suspect one, have your vet take a scraping of the affected skin and examine it under a microscope. Only he can determine which type it is.

Ear Mange (Otodectic), sometimes called canker, is caused by rather large mites which infect the ear canal, causing painful irritation. The dog repeatedly shakes his head and scratches, crying and whining meanwhile. Soak a layer of cotton in mineral oil, wrap it around your index finger, and clean the ear with this gently.

There are many excellent cures for ear canker but scrupulous cleanliness helps most of all. The dark discharge has a heavy unpleasant smell which will warn you of the mite's presence if the dog's misery and scratching at the base of the ear has not already pointed it out. Quite often a dog has been deemed "crabby" or shy when all that ailed him was ear mange.

Sarcoptic mange: This is greatly to be dreaded as it takes three months or longer to cure, and involves medicated baths and lotions. Red, angry patches with crusts on them are found on the inner sides of the flanks, belly and legs. In warm weather the skin exudes a stale, mouse-like smell. The irritation is considerable. Sarcoptic mange should be placed under professional care at ounce,

Demodectic mange is not too common. It usually manifests itself on the face, head, or legs in bare patches with the affected skin dark in color and very thin and poor. It, too, is difficult to treat and may take several months to clear up. Bitches can pass this ailment on to their litters even though they appear healthy themselves. Professional treatment required.

Nursing

First, you must learn to take your Poodle's temperature. The normal temperature of a dog is 101.5°, but this can vary a point or two without causing anxiety. A puppy's temperature can easily be 102° if he has been scampering about. But anything above 102.5°, or below 100°, in either adult or puppy, should give rise to some anxiety.

There is one exception, and that is in the female who is within 24 hours of producing her litter, for then her temperature may be below 100°.

The thermometer should be the blunt ended type. Be sure to shake the mercury well down to below 98° before using it. Lubricate the silvered end of the thermometer with petroleum jelly, hold your Poodle with his head under your left arm, with your elbow pressing his right side; with your left hand, hold up his tail. With your right hand, insert the lubricated end of the thermometer a little way up the rectum. Do not use force. The thermometer should slip into the rectum easily for about two inches. Keep hold of your Poodle, allowing the thermometer to remain in position for at least one minute. Then gently withdraw it and make your reading.

You should also check your dog's pulse. To do this, place your hand on his abdomen and slide your fingers into the groin, where the hind leg joins the abdomen. Press your finger on to the inside of the thigh bone and you will feel the femoral artery pulsing. Small dogs have a faster pulse rate than large dogs, so you will find that small Toy Poodles have a pulse rate of about 90 to the minute, while Miniature Poodles Run at about 80 a minute, and Standards at about 70. If the Poodle is unwell, the pulse may register from 120 to 160 beats to the minute, or may be as low as 40 beats. A dog's pulse is not entirely regular, as is that of a human being, and will be intermittent, but you will find there is a pattern in the irregularity and you should get to know this pattern by counting the pulse now and again when your Poodle is quite well.

Administering Medicine

You must also learn how to give various medicines. When administering liquid medicines, the Poodle, if a small one, should be placed on a table; if bigger, on the floor. With your left hand, pull the right-hand corner of the dog's lips outwards, making a small pouch. The medicine should then be poured into the pouch from a spoon or small bottle, and his head raised immediately so that the liquid will trickle down his throat. The mouth should be held shut until all the liquid has been swallowed, and to induce him to swallow, his throat may be stroked.

Tablets or capsules may sometimes be satisfactorily hidden in a small piece of meat to be unsuspectingly swallowed by the Poodle.

To administer pills, grasp the upper jaw with the left hand at the hinge. Gently ease open the mouth, and push the tablet down using the index and center finger of the right hand.

A few bites should be fed first so that he is not suspicious. If this is not possible, place the Poodle between your knees, open his mouth wide and put the pill on the back of his tongue and gently shove it down his throat. Close his mouth immediately and stroke his throat until you feel him swallow. When powders are to be given, they, too, may be disguised in a piece of meat; otherwise, the mouth should be opened and the powder shaken onto the back of the tongue.

Peace and Quiet

Dogs who become ill instinctively seek out a quiet place which is usually dark and deserted. Such conditions allow them to sleep undisturbed hidden from their enemies until the illness has passed. This is the natural way for the dog to find his own healing. Therefore, when your dog is suffering from some illness, find a secluded, quiet place where he can have his bed. An empty room is one of the most suitable places; be quite sure that no other dogs can get near him to upset and worry him. If possible, place his bed in a dark corner, or at any rate not in the full sunlight, or where any bright light is upon him. Dogs always avoid bright light when they are ill. It will probably be necessary to have a bright light for examination purposes, or when dressings are to be applied, but at other times, keep him in a dark corner.

Also be careful about noise; enter the sick room quietly. There should be a pronounced muted atmosphere about the room. At this time, your Poodle will doze a great deal, and at times will even sleep deeply. It is extremely important that he be awakened slowly. Stroke him gently and talk softly to him, until he is fully awake, and only raise him to minister to him. If there is more than one person in the room, their voices should be kept low, never loud and upsetting. Disturb him as little as is conducive to necessary cleanliness. The quieter you can be, the more chance the seriously ill dog has of regaining his health.

Warmth

The sick dog needs to be kept warm, but not so hot that he is uncomfortable. Since he is not getting any excercise, and so not generating much heat, he will naturally not be as warm as usual unless he is running a temperature. The best means of heat in the sick room is probably the use of an infra-red lamp, for this can be suspended above the sick bed, and raised or lowered according to the temperature required.

A room thermometer should be laid on the Poodle's back from time to time to check that the correct amount of heat is getting to the dog. The room temperature should read about a steady 65° to 70° fahrenheit. If a lamp is used, the heat is radiated onto the place required, and the whole room does not need to be heated. There should be fresh air circulating, but all drafts should be avoided. At a time like this, the Poodle needs every ounce of energy to combat the disease, and he must not have to waste any of that energy keeping warm.

Beware of an electrically heated pad or blanket in or under the dog's bed unless it is one of the rubberized type specifically designed for dogs, because when seriously ill he may have little control over his natural functions, and liquid could cause him to be electrocuted. Make your Poodle as comfortable as possible by giving him a soft bed with a rug or blanket against his back. If you can give him a circular bed, so much the better, as this will fit his shape, and there will be no hard corners pressing into him.

Cleanliness

It goes almost without saying that cleanliness is of paramount importance. All dishes, spoons, and containers must be well washed before being used, and even more so after use. All soiled paper, cotton or dressings must be burned immediately. Wear a clean apron or coat when attending to the sick Poodle, and be careful to wash your hands before and after touching him or carrying out any treatment.

While the Poodle himself must be kept clean, try to disturb him as little as possible. If he does not fancy any food or drink that you may offer him, do not leave it lying around to become dry or tainted. Keep his eyes, and his mouth, and his underparts clean. If he is feverish, his eyes may need lubricating from time to time, for he will become dehydrated, and so his eyelids will get hot and stiff. A desperately ill dog may not even have the strength to drink. In this case, a piece of cotton should be soaked in clean cold water and then squeezed out onto his tongue or into his mouth. He will appreciate this very much indeed, and it can save him from severe dehydration. This moistening should be carried out every 15 minutes or so until the crisis has passed. His mouth and nose should be frequently sponged with tepid water to which has been added a squeeze of lemon juice. His underparts can also be sponged with water and a very mild disinfectant or antiseptic lotion. Do not leave him damp; dry him gently with a soft towel or cotton.

Regular Routine

Although this is mentioned last, it is by no means the least important. Try to carry out all attentions to the sick dog at regular intervals; in between, leave him alone and quiet, so that he may rest and relax. It is not at all good for him to be fussed over with treatment or ministration every five minutes or so.

Most food or medicine is usually given every four hours. This is a usual interval, and the sick dog should have everything done for him in the same order. By this is meant that first he should have his temperature checked (although this is usually only necessary night and morning), then be taken to relieve himself if he is well enough to go outside; next he should have any dressings attended to, medicines given; meanwhile his bed should be straightened and renewed if necessary. Then his food should be fed, followed by any cleaning of face and underparts. Then as quickly as possible, let him get back into his bed, and sleep for the next four hours undisturbed.

If the Poodle is seriously ill, it may be necessary to attend him at least once during the night. Be sure that all medicines, bottles of tablets, and so on are clearly labelled, so that there is no danger of error. If you are able to work out a careful four-hour routine, carrying out each ministration in the same order, you will find this helps the Poodle's recovery, because he will know exactly what to expect and when to expect it.

It is particularly important to give medicine at correct intervals, especially in the case of antibiotics and drugs, for an overlap in time may cause a bad build-up. Equally, going too long without medicine may detract from the alleviation of pain, and allow germs to regain their hold. So keep to a strict routine.

Nursing Aids

There are several nursing aids which will prove useful. One is a linen bag, to keep the Poodle from scratching or biting some wound, or irritating a sore place. If the Poodle is small, a pillow case can be utilized; if not, a larger bag must be made. A drawstring is fixed around the top, the Poodle popped into the bag, and the string pulled up around his neck and tied to his collar. This is particularly good nursing aid for use at night, for once in the bag, the Poodle cannot really walk far and can only shuffle about, and it will prevent him from licking, chewing or biting himself while you, yourself, are sleeping. Most Poodles, after the first few minutes, will bear with this sort of restraint quite philosophically.

Another convenient aid is a stocking cap which can be used if the Poodle has ear trouble. Cut off a nylon stocking to just above the ankle, and then cut off the toe piece. Slip this light cap over his ears, with his nose poked through the toe hole. By this means, dressings can be kept in place; the cap itself is so light that the Poodle is not worried by it. It is extremely useful for keeping the ears close to the head when it is necessary to prevent the wind from blow-

A cardboard collar, often called an "Elizabethan Ruff." This is used, among other things, to keep the Poodle from chewing off a dressing.

to the head when it is necessary to prevent the wind from blowing into the dog's ear canal. It has a happier use, too, for it can be slipped over the Poodle's head during a clipping session, since it is often difficult to keep the ear fringes out of the way of the scissors when trimming feet or anklets.

Another helpful aid is a stiff cardboard collar called an Elizabethan Ruff laced up with either string or bandage. This is a preventative measure used only when it is impossible by any other means to prevent the Poodle from biting some wound or eruption on his body.

A light weight coat is often useful to keep dressings in place; one made from linen or some soft washable material is especially helpful in cases of abdominal operations. The coat fastens with ties along the top of the back, and keeps the dog from scratching a wound or a scar. It is also good for a Pneumonia coat. For cases where the chest has to be kept warm, a warm and soft woolen material should be used.

An overlay of plastic or polyethylene is useful when either sewn or tied onto the top of a warm dog coat. It may become necessary for the Poodle to go out in the pouring rain, and an overlay such as this will keep him from getting wet and chilled; it will also obviate the difficulty of drying a thick blanket coat.

It is hoped that the majority of Poodle owners will never have to cope with a serious illness, but that if they do, the foregoing suggestions should help them to nurse their Poodle to a speedy recovery.

Finally, it is really essential to keep up a cheerful attitude in the canine sick room. Poodles are extremely sensitive to environment, and if the owner is anxious, fearful and pessimistic over the outcome of the illness, the Poodle will sense this unhappy attitude. On the other hand, if the owner continually reassures the Poodle that he is a good dog, that all is for the best, and that he is going to get well – he will do just that!

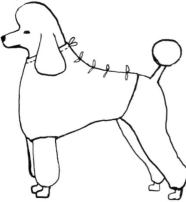

A lightweight coat is often useful to keep dressings in place. The coat fastens with ties along the top of the back and keeps the dog from scratching a wound or a scar.

The companion clip keeps your pet Poodle looking neat around the house and requires a minimum of care,

XIX First Aid

First aid, as the name implies, means action in emergency. It does not mean professional treatment or diagnosis. Accidents happen without warning, and unless some measure of first aid is applied, the Poodle is likely to suffer unnecessary pain, and indeed, may even die from lack of immediate attention. You should know what to do immediately. There is not time to look up directions in a book, or thumb an index. May we suggest that as a Poodle owner you completely familiarize yourself with the first aid treatments given here for such emergencies as fractures, asphyxiation, drowning, poisoning, burns, electric shock, and road accidents.

The First Aid Kit

Every dog should have his own first aid kit. On it should be the telephone number of your veterinarian, and it might be wise to have the phone number of a second vet in case your regular man is not available. The equipment and medical supplies to be stored in such a metal container are optional but we recommend the following as minimum:

Smelling salts	String for tourniquet
Vinegar	Potassium permanganate
Brandy – clearly labeled	Bandages
Bicarbonate of soda	Crepe bandage (3 inch)
Dextrose in a polyethylene bag	Wound dressings
Sedative tablets	Adhesive tape (medicated)
Rock salt	Curved scissors
Washing soda (lumps)	Tweezers
Burn ointment	Cotton

Restraint

If your Poodle is hurt or frightened, he may act unpredictably snapping and biting. Restraint will be needed. Be prepared for this likely change of disposition, for you will not be of much use in an emergency if you too need treatment for dog bite! It may be necessary to apply a muzzle, and to do this, take a piece of four inch bandaging about 24 inches long; twist this into a noose and slip it over the Poodle's nose, then draw the ends fairly tightly under his chin and tie around the back of the neck. This may not always keep him from biting but it will make it difficult for him to do so, and will at any rate give you time to avoid his teeth. If it is necessary to restrain him still further, you may have to use a piece of bandaging to tie his fore and hind legs together. If he is hysterical and panic stricken, a rug or coat held over his head will help, while you hold him tightly, endeavoring to reassure him with a soothing voice.

Giving an Emetic

It is sometimes necessary to empty the contents of the dog's stomach. Thus something must be used to induce him to vomit. The simplest emetics are either salt and water, mustard and water or a 3% solution of hydrogen peroxide and water, 50-50, poured down the throat via the lip-pocket method; others are a piece of ordinary washing soda or a small piece of soap to be put down the throat. Vomiting will take place shortly.

Poodle bag to prevent scratching or licking of wounds, or tearing of dressings.

A temporary muzzle made out of a piece of bandage. It is looped under the chin and tied at the back of the neck.

Using an Enema

The type of enema syringe used for a child is suitable for a Poodle. Prepare half to two teaspoonsful of glycerine in one to four ounces of warm water. Lubricate the syringe nozzle and insert well into the rectum of the dog. Squeeze in the fluid *very slowly,* and withdraw the syringe quickly, at the same time firmly holding a pad of cotton over the anus for half a minute. Remove the pad and maneuver the Poodle so that his rear parts are lower than his head; the fluid will flow out bringing with it any clogging feces. It is best to carry out this operation with the Poodle lying on his side, holding up the rear parts while the enema is being given.

237

Artificial Respiration

A difficult thing to do, but to know how may well be the means of saving your Poodle's life. The method is to lay the dog on his side, then place one or both hands depending on the dog's size, over the area of the chest, and slowly and rhythmically depress and release. This should be carried out more or less in time with your own breathing, or approximately twenty times to the minute. The secret lies in carrying out the task gently and rhythmically, as any rough or jerking movement will not bring success.

"Kiss of Life"

This is another highly successful method of bringing the dog back to life. The idea is hold the Poodle's mouth closed, and to place your own mouth completely over his mouth and nostrils. Breathe in and out normally for as long as possible without taking your mouth away. Again, time the action to your own breathing, at about twenty breaths to the minute. It is an exhausting method of resuscitation, but singularly successful with those newborn puppies who fail to commence breathing at birth.

Applying a Tourniquet

In cases of severe external bleeding from a leg wound, a tourniquet is often the only answer. If the spurting blood is bright red, it means that an artery has been injured; in this case, the tourniquet must be applied *above* the wound, in fact, between the wound and the heart. But blood that is dark red and oozing profusely indicates an injured vein, and the pressure must be applied below the wound, on the side away from the heart.

In an emergency, anything will do as a tourniquet – a piece of string, a bandage, a dog lead. Whatever is used should be tied tightly around the limb, and then, to create the necessary pressure, a stick, pencil or a fork should be pushed into the knot and twisted, creating pressure until the bleeding stops. But the tourniquet must be loosened every ten minutes for half a minute and then pressure resumed otherwise tissues will be damaged. If the Poodle being taken to the veterinarian has had a tourniquet applied, a note to this effect should be attached to the dog.

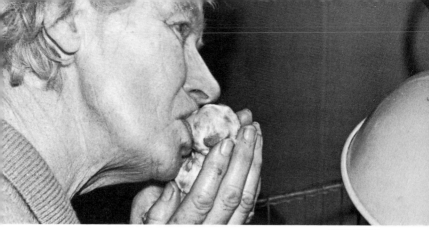

The "Kiss of life." A highly successful method of artificial respiration.

Pressure Bandage

This is not quite so drastic as a tourniquet, but if applied properly it will staunch the flow of blood; it may be left on longer than a tourniquet without harming the tissues. Apply a thick pad to the bleeding wound and then wrap it around *very tightly* with a fairly wide bandage, and either tie the ends securely or use wide adhesive tape. Such a bandage may be left on undisturbed for up to twenty minutes at a time.

Shock

Treatment for shock plays an important part in nearly all cases of accident, sudden pain, fright, or where there is excessive loss of blood. A Poodle suffering from shock will show a very feeble pulse, slow heart beat and extremely shallow breathing. If these symptoms are apparent, keep him as warm as possible. The best way to do this is to cover him with coats or rugs, put hot water bottles at his back and by his feet, but be careful that the hot bottles are wrapped so that there can be no danger of burns. The Poodle should be kept quiet and in a darkened room. If he is in a state of collapse, smelling salts applied to the nostrils will help, and if fully conscious, a few drops of brandy will stimulate him temporarily. But brandy should not be given if there is severe bleeding.

Now we will deal with the sudden emergencies that need immediate action. These are all situations that *could* occur at any time, but, on the other hand, may never happen in the Poodle's life.

For show ring training, the Poodle is never too young to start. The first lesson begins at the age of 8 weeks.

Asphyxia or Strangulation

A condition when the dog cannot breathe because air cannot reach his lungs. This can happen in cases of coal gas poisoning, choking, drowning, or accidental hanging. In cases of asphyxiation from fumes or coal gas poisoning, fresh air is essential, and the Poodle should be removed with the least possible delay from the gas filled area and laid on the ground out of doors. The air around him should be fanned to create a good current, and people should be kept from crowding around and impeding the fresh air supply. Smelling salts held under the dog's nose will help restore breathing.

Choking

This may be on a large chunk of biscuit or meat. Try to hook out the offending object with your forefinger; if this is impossible, try to push it down the throat past the narrow part. A smart pat or thump on the back will help, and if it's a small dog, raise him by his hind legs, with head hanging down, and give him a good shaking. Desperate situations call for desperate measures!

Drowning

A small dog may be turned upside down and shaken, but a large Poodle should be laid on a steep slope with head hanging down, in an effort to get the water out of the lungs. Artificial respiration or the "Kiss of Life" should be employed. When he begins to show signs of recovery, rub him briskly with warm towels, and keep him very warm and dry, preferably under an infra-red heat lamp.

Hanging

This can sometimes happen if a dog is tied to the steering wheel of an automobile and the window is left open, or if left tied up on a table or chair. Immediately loosen the leash, and again apply artificial respiration or the "Kiss of Life."

Burns

For burns of all types, the best treatment is cold water. The main damage from burns is the continued heat damage to the tissues. Thus, swabbing with cold water for several minutes will reduce the heat in the area and lessen the severity of the burn. If it is possible, direct the jet of cold water from the tap directly onto the burned area. Cold tea, of vinegar and water in equal proportions, is useful in all types of alkali burns. For acid burns, which may well be in the mouth and on the tongue, use bicarbonate of soda in the proportion of two teaspoonsful to a cup of cold water. Swab the burned parts liberally for several minutes.

Electric Shock

A not too uncommon occurrence, especially with puppies, as it is often caused by chewing through an electric wire. Do not touch the dog with your bare hands, as you may also receive the shock. First, disconnect the wire at the source. If this is impossible, push the animal out of the way of the live wire or object, using a stick or piece of wood or any other non-conducting material. Once the Poodle has been removed from the area of danger, treat the burns in the normal way; cover him with rugs or coats, and give him a warm drink as he will be suffering from excessive shock.

Fractures

Owing to their diminutive size and fairy-like structure, many Toy Poodles fracture a fore or hind leg. It can happen so easily, through running down a passage and hitting a table leg, by jumping awkwardly off a chair or table, or, of course, in road accidents. The Poodle will give a rending scream which will, after a second or two, turn into a pathetic whining. The break will be excessively painful and the dog may attempt to bite all and sundry.

Puppies often sustain what is known as a "green stick fracture", which is like a severe bend with perhaps an accompanying crack in the length of the bone. The other kinds are: a. simple fracture, which is a straight break through the bone or bones; b. compound fracture, when besides the fracture of the bone, the tissues and skin are also torn, frequently exposing the bone; c. comminuted, when the bone is crushed into several pieces.

It is usually obvious when a fracture has been sustained because the leg is deformed. But if no deformity or lump can be seen or felt, an easy test is to squeeze the upper part of the leg; normally, this will cause the dog to flex his muscles and stretch his leg. If he can still do this, the leg is not broken, but if there is no reflex action, and part of the leg seems to be drooping, a fracture of some kind has probably occurred. The first aid treatment lies in keeping the limb as rigid as possible until veterinary aid can be obtained, and a regular splint, or plaster applied. First, cover the leg with cotton, and then wind several thicknesses of corrugated paper or cardboard around the leg. To give further support, place two sticks or pieces of wood on either side of the leg on top of the cardboard, and tie the whole fairly tightly with strips of bandage,

The Poodle, if small enough, can be held in the arms to prevent further damage to the leg, but a large Poodle should be made to lie on the ground, or a rug, on the side opposite the injured leg, and restrained in that position with the leg supported on a coat or cushion. No food or drink should be given as an anesthetic may be necessary. Treat as for shock.

Heat Stroke

This usually entails excessive distress ending in total collapse. The Poodle must be moved immediately to a cool and shaded place. His head, the back of his neck, and his abdomen should be sponged with cold water. Make sure that a current of cool air reaches him, and prevent onlookers from crowding in. Fan with a newspaper.

Poisoning

This covers a wide field as there are a great many substances which may cause poisoning. As a general rule it is important to induce the dog to expel the contents of his stomach with the least possible delay, and to do this an emetic to make him vomit must be given. Peroxide and water (50-50), salt, soda, soap and mustard are all excellent emetics.

If the Poodle has swallowed an alkaloid poison such as morphine, heroin, or cocaine, a weak solution of permanganate of potash should be used. If the poison is a corrosive of caustic *alkali*, then give vinegar or citric acid, but if a corrosive *acid*, give an alkali such as bicarbonate of soda or soda water. In arsenic poisoning, an immediate emetic is needed, followed by milk to drink, and a strong purgative medicine. For food poisoning, also give an emetic, and a purge, and afterwards a bland diet and plenty of honey and milk. Lead poisoning which often is the result of licking or chewing painted objects, calls for an emetic, then milk and honey. For phosphorus poisoning, use an emetic of peroxide and water (50-50) but on no account give milk or any fatty substance. Honey and water is excellent.

Road Accidents

A Poodle hit by an automobile suffers a great deal from fright, and may very well turn on anyone who tries to help him. If possible, take him firmly by the scruff of the neck and soothe him in a gentle, reassuring voice with quiet stroking. If he does not get up of his own accord, he should not be moved unless traffic makes it essential, for he may have internal injuries causing hemorrhage. Frequently, however, it may be only a case of bruises and fright, but there is no way of telling until a veterinarian makes an examination.

The dog will undoubtedly be suffering from shock to a greater or lesser degree; so keep him warm with blankets or coat. No liquids of any kind should be given as he may have to have an anesthetic later on. If there are obvious fractures, keep the limb as immobile as possible. If any bad gash is bleeding profusely, hold a pad firmly on the wound until help arrives. If a limb is bleeding badly, a tourniquet may have to be applied. In a road accident, when the extent of injuries cannot really be assessed, the main concern is to stop any further injury by immobilization, to try to staunch any excessive bleeding, and to comfort and reassure the Poodle until professional help arrives.

Convulsions

Before the days of vaccination, it was not uncommon for puppies and adult dogs to go into convulsions, but nowadays this is unusual. However, such convulsions or "fits" may occur for very different reasons. They may be symptoms of epilepsy, or poisoning, or the onset of a virus disease, and in puppies may be the result of teething or sudden indigestion because the puppy has swallowed large lumps of food too quickly, or they can be caused by the presence of worms.

There are two points to notice. First, if the Poodle remains conscious and aware of his surroundings, but cannot control his movements, and has a desperate jerking, pedaling movement of his legs, and a certain amount of salivation with champing of the jaws, this usually points to a toxic condition in his system. Keep him from damaging himself, but don't attempt to pick him up. Just let the convulsion wear itself out. Cold water on his head and the back of his neck will help. A "fit" of this sort is usually over in a minute or two, and then the Poodle will shake himself and appear rather vague and dizzy, but this will pass. A visit to the veterinarian will probably reveal the cause,

If, on the other hand, the Poodle loses consciousness and is obviously unaware of his surroundings, it is more serious, and he will not "come around" in a short period. He may become completely rigid and stiff, while his eyes will be upturned and will show the whites; his jaws will probably be working in a chewing attitude, and he may pass water or defecate. This is a case for the immediate attention of the veterinarian, as it could mean brain damage of viral origin. This type of convulsion, or series of convulsions, occasionally happens to a dog who is recovering from a severe virus infection; suddenly, just as he appears to be almost well again, the brain may become affected, and Encephalitis set in. The outlook in such cases is not a happy one. While the Poodle is unconscious, awaiting the arrival of veterinary help, cover him with a blanket, and if possible, pull his tongue out of the side of his mouth, so that it does not hinder his breathing.

The foregoing are all measures calling for immediate action. There are many minor ailments or situations which may also need treatment, but these do not, strictly speaking, come under the heading of first aid, because no further treatment will, in most cases, be needed.

Splinters and thorns need attention; if the foreign body can be located, it should be removed by tweezers, and the part then soaked in warm water to which has been added a small amount of disinfectant.

Cuts caused by barbed wire, or jagged ends of metal, should be bathed with warm water and a safe antiseptic, and then either a dry dressing or some healing ointment should be applied.

Fish hooks can be a danger, but do not try to pull them out. The correct way is to cut off the shank and then draw the hook forward and out; again bathe and apply a soothing ointment.

Dogs occasionally suffer from small boils or abscesses, quite often on the anus. The cause may be clogged anal glands. A stiff injection of penicillin, or one of its variants, usually takes the pain out of such eruptions, bringing them to a head in a matter of hours. Hot compresses will help, and when the abscess bursts, the pus should be swabbed away with warm water and disinfectant. It takes some time before the abscess drains completely, so it will need attention at least three times a day for two or three days.

Small cuts or snips suffered by the Poodle while being clipped may bleed profusely. On any but white or apricot Poodles, fine crystals of permanganate of potash may be pressed into the wound; the bleeding will cease immediately. However, the crystals do stain, turning everything to a violent purple when they come in contact with a wet or damp substance. Adrenalin which your veterinarian may inject is another good chemical for staunching blood, and this does not stain.

In conclusion, we would like to repeat that the keynote to all first aid is to be prepared, know where everything is, know exactly what to do, and do it quickly.

German Champion BB Kölsch-Inglisch, bred and owned by Frau Bruns-wicker of Köln, Germany.

XX   Care of the Old Poodle

There is a popular theory, not scientifically true, that each year of a dog's life equals seven years of a human life. Thus, a ten year old dog is the equivalent of a man who has attained the age of seventy, and coming to the end of his allotted span of "three score years and ten." However, in these days of advanced medical science, man's expectation of life is greater than it used to be, and possibly the same applies to the dog. Some breeds are known to have short lives, but the Poodle is a breed which is long-lived, and it is by no means unusual to find a Poodle attaining the fine old age of 17 or 18 years, although 14 years is the more usual span.

But certainly from the age of 12 onwards, our beloved Poodle will need extra care, additional comforts, and a peaceful atmosphere for his last years.

It always comes as a shock when we notice that our old friend is beginning to slow up, and we realize that he is getting old. The years pass so quickly. It seems only yesterday that he was gangling puppy, and now here is, just a little hard of hearing, more than a little shortsighted, inclined to be greedy and putting on more weight than he should, rather stiff when he gets up in the mornings, and inclined to be a little short-tempered with children and other dogs.

We now owe it to him to make these last few years, or maybe only months, as peaceful and comfortable as possible.

His defective hearing will not worry him too much; in fact, it may even benefit him, for the noisy sounds of modern life will now be a little muffled. But his lack of hearing may well be an irritation to his owner, for the old Poodle will not hear when he is called, and this means that he will have to be fetched from wherever he happens to be. It is now important to handle him very gently; just touch him to attract his attention and show him where he is to go. He must not be shouted at, nor touched or pushed suddenly, and never from behind, for this will make him jump and cause his heart to race – not a very good thing for an old dog.

Failing eyesight will slow down his movements considerably. He must know where things are, and such things as his bed, his water bowl and other possessions must not be moved from place to place. If he is taken to visit a strange place, he must be kept on a leash and gently led, so that he does not injure himself by knocking into doors, furniture, strange people and strange dogs.

His appetite may well increase far beyond what is good for him, and while he must not suffer from hunger, he must not be allowed to increase his weight, weakening his heart. So his diet must be well-planned, and any fattening items like cookies, cake, chocolate drops, and so forth, must be strictly rationed, while a diet high in proteins will keep him in good condition. To stave off the pangs of hunger, the old Poodle will appreciate two or three small meals a day rather than one large one. Do not forget that the food must be soft and digestible, for his teeth are not as sound as they once were. Be punctual with his meals for they are now his chief interest.

Arthritis and muscular pains often trouble the elderly Poodle, and he may be very stiff in the mornings or when he wakes from a nap. He may find steps or stairs a difficulty; in this case, a small ramp will help. His bed must be positioned out of any draft, in a really warm and comfortable corner of the room. See that he has a foam mattress, and a warm rug to nestle in, for he is bound to feel chilly on cold days, and it is then that his old bones will begin to ache.

Protect him from the exuberant high spirits of both young children and young puppies. He may have loved both, but in his declining years they may excite and confuse him, and although he will not mean it, he will appear irascible and short-tempered. So help him to get away from the lightheartedness of youth.

Finally, keep him tidy and clean, but don't worry him too often with shampooing and clipping sessions. His figure will probably have spread a little, and so an ultra-chic coiffure is no longer essential.

If such care and consideration is given to your old Poodle, he will have the peaceful and contented old age that he so richly deserves.

But there will come the time when most reluctantly you realize that he has become a burden to himself; you will then have to render him that one last service of a peaceful, unwaking sleep. He may be in pain for which there is no relief; he may have become senile and unable to find his way about; he may have become incontinent and this will distress him greatly, for he will always have been scrupulously clean in his habits. You must face the fact that it is no longer kind to let him drag on in misery.

When this moment of decision comes, the owner must not shirk his duty. If he loves his Poodle, he will not. The old dog must not be asked to face death alone or in the hands of strangers. The owner, or someone the old Poodle knows well and loves, should be with him to hold him and reassure him when the moment comes for him to be put to sleep. For then the words "put to sleep" will have their true meaning, and our old dog will only think it as another bedtime, and will not realize it is the sleep from which he will not wake. Don't avoid this last service to your Poodle even though you may feel you cannot bear it, that it will make *you* suffer too much. It is little enough to render him in return for all those years of faithful companionship.

We have followed our Poodle from puppyhood to old age. Maybe we have had the pleasure of breeding litters of puppies, or of seeing him take top honors in the show ring, or in the obedience field; maybe he has just been a wonderful companion, sympathizing with us when we were sad, rejoicing when we were happy. But whatever our Poodle has been to us, we have come to realize that there is no other breed of dog which could have given us such devotion and loyalty, which could have had such a delightful sense of humor, and which could have possessed such tremendous intelligence.

A toast to the King of Dogs – the Poodle! If only he could live forever!

END